Neighbors & Neighborhoods

Elements of Successful Community Design

Sidney Brower

The Citizens Planning Series

For ~~Ralph~~ with best wishes *Sidney*

APA

American Planning Association
Planners Press

Making Great Communities Happen

Chicago | Washington, D.C.

205 N. Michigan Ave., Suite 1200, Chicago, IL 60601-5927
1030 15th St., NW, Suite 750W, Washington, DC 20005-1503

www.planning.org/plannerspress

ISBN: 978-1-61190-001-9

Library of Congress Control Number 2011909374

This project was supported by a grant to the author from the
Graham Foundation for Advanced Study in the Fine Arts. It was
also supported by the School of Architecture, Planning, and
Preservation at the University of Maryland.

Design and typesetting by Scribe, Inc. (www.scribenet.com)

Printed in the United States of America

For Cynthia, Kate, and Gideon

CONTENTS

PART 3: COMMUNITY DESIGN

LIST OF ILLUSTRATIONS

FOREWORD

Parris N. Glendening

In 1997 when Maryland adopted the nation's first statewide comprehensive smart growth program, everything seemed relatively simple and straightforward. We knew what we were for and what we were against. We wanted strong, revitalized cities and communities. We supported protecting open space and farmland. We pushed transit and transit-oriented development. We wanted economically diverse, inclusive, and prosperous communities, each with a strong sense of place. Our enemies were obvious: low-density sprawl, more roads, and cookie-cutter subdivisions.

As we moved to implement the laws, regulations, and policies needed to realize the smart growth visions, the contradictions and inconsistencies of trying to apply a statewide program to diverse local communities quickly became clear. We sought economically and racially diverse communities, but many otherwise successful smart growth revitalizations were correctly challenged as gentrification in a different form. In some cases, the poor and longtime residents were simply "moved out." Likewise, the early goals of many "rediscovered neighborhoods" often focused on landing those "symbols of arrival"—the Starbucks, the Whole Foods, et cetera. These new arrivals come at a cost, though, often forcing longtime neighborhood nonfranchise businesses to close.

Furthermore, increasing vitality in existing communities often requires increasing development densities. Even if smart growth aims only to return a community to its historic density, though, opposition from residents can be intense. Even in the face of vacant storefronts and abandoned residential properties, people often fear and resist efforts to increase densities. These are just a few of the many tensions that arise from the implementation of smart growth programs.

Understanding and adjusting to these contradictions, inconsistencies, and community responses are essential not only for successful implementation of smart growth, planning, and design principles—as well as for the future of the smart growth and sustainability movements—but also for the future of *communities* themselves.

The major demographics of contemporary America compel us to resolve these tensions that arise in bringing smart growth strategies to existing communities. With expected national population growth of over 100 million in the next 30 years, the graying and browning of America, and, for the first time, a majority of our households being headed by a single person, we cannot continue the current development patterns, spreading most of our new growth across the landscape. This is particularly so if we envision communitywide prosperity, in livable, walkable communities embedded in a green and sustainable environment.

But how do we resolve these conflicts? *Neighbors and Neighborhoods* highlights one major portion of the answer. Communities are different, gloriously different. Some have long histories embedded in every corner of the community. Others have developer-manufactured "histories," as in the mysterious case of Opa-locka, Florida, discussed in Chapter 5.

Likewise, differences in area, population size, community experiences, population homogeneity, culture, legal structure, and so many other variables make each community unique and present implementation challenges for smart growth leaders, planners, and design professionals. As you read here of the many different communities and talk with residents in open-ended interviews you will surely see, as I have, the importance of clearly understanding a community before attempting to design its future.

Smart growth or sustainability efforts must be adapted to the uniqueness of the existing community. An expectation that a community can be forced into an inflexible mold of a rigid statewide law or program will almost certainly be frustrated or end in failure. The great diversity of community illustrated here in places as different as Locust Point or Pigtown in Baltimore, and Carmel, California, and Levittown, New York, and Riverside, Illinois, reinforces this conclusion. For me, these chapters produce not a breakthrough "Aha!" moment but a clearer and reinforced appreciation of earlier insights and observations.

These observations in turn are filtered through my own political experiences. My first real exposure to the sources of the strength of a community occurred when I was elected to the Hyattsville, Maryland, City Council in 1973. For many people in Maryland and the Washington, D.C., area, Hyattsville was simply an ugly stretch of U.S. 1 just outside the District of Columbia, filled with used-car lots and many empty storefronts. What most people did not see was the viable community of 15,000 people, with a history going back to 1859. They missed the strong institutions such as St. Jerome's Catholic Church, where many residents were married, expected to see their children married, and eventually anticipated family funeral services.

Hyattsville High School (later a middle school) served a similar role, having graduated three generations of local business and civic leadership. There were the less formal organizations, such as the Hyattsville Volunteer Fire Department, which not only helped to protect the community but also linked young men (and later women) with the community "old guard," which seemed to have a constant presence at the station. Stewarding all of this was an extraordinary group of political leaders who held office for decades and routinely rose to higher offices such as Speaker of the House for the State Legislature (Perry Wilkinson), U.S. congressman (Hervey Machen), and county executive (Win Kelly and me). Together, these are the forces that gave Hyattsville its strength. They are also the forces that give meaning and direction to the communities observed in this book. The impact of their absence, as Sidney Brower notes, can be felt as clearly as their presence.

After serving eight years on the Prince George's County Council, I was fortunate to be elected county executive in 1982. Most people in the metropolitan area thought of Prince George's as simply the populous county adjacent to Washington, D.C., with the nation's largest suburban African-American population.

To me it is much more. The county is a wonderful mosaic of diverse communities. There are communities like the Town of Bladensburg, which traces its roots to 1732, when it served briefly as a tobacco port, and which witnessed nationally historic events like the Battle of Bladensburg, which preceded the burning of Washington in the War of 1812. Bladensburg is also the site of the infamous Dueling Grounds, which saw among many others the Stephen Decatur/James Barron duel (1820).

Other towns have a more recent but equally proud history. Greenbelt, for example, was one of three Green Towns first proposed by Rexford Guy Tugwell in 1935 and laid out and championed thereafter by Eleanor Roosevelt. Tugwell's idealistic, almost utopian, goal was to use Depression-era public works programs to create a largely self-contained and self-sufficient community. Residents today fight to hold onto this tradition, by protecting not only the original structures, pathways, and parks but also the ideals of the original settlement. Through community festivals, parades, farmers markets, and co-ops, Greenbelt sustains a high level of civic activism. There is, for example, a consumers co-op grocery store. The local newspaper, the *Greenbelt News Review,* is also a co-op. Greenbelt is often cited as one of the most progressive places in the state. The idealism of Greenbelt is echoed in this book in places like Lake Claire Commons in Atlanta, or the Twin Oaks Community in Louisa, Virginia, the latter inspired by the ideas of behaviorist B. F. Skinner.

Areas like Mitchellville, Maryland, just outside the Capital Beltway, are home to some of the wealthiest predominately African-American communities in the nation. A few miles down the road is the Town of Bowie, much of which was an early, and then almost all-white, Levittown.

Why the quick journey into the communities of Prince George's County and the side trip into the political life of Parris Glendening? It is because these communities and what I learned from them are cousins to the many communities covered by Sidney Brower in this book. The lessons they offer are the same. Brower's emerge from serious academic and field research; mine evolved from personal and political observations.

If we are to be successful using community design to create or strengthen a community and implement smart growth plans or sustainability programs, we must first understand the community. We must understand the history, the people, the culture, and so much more about what makes that community what it is, how it can sustain itself, and how it can prosper. Then and only then will good design work.

Last, good design must involve the community on a continuing basis. Columbia, Maryland, created by famed planner and developer James Rouse, is offered herein as an example of that continuous involvement, ongoing even today as Columbia adds significant additional density to its Town Center. Celebration, Florida, created in 1996 by the Walt Disney Company, is offered as an example of the opposite approach—top down corporate decision making with very little community involvement and, not surprisingly, very different results.

If we rely on good design alone to create walkable, livable places, to create community, or to advance smart growth, we cannot fully achieve our visions. Likewise, if we rely only on understanding the community without adding good design, we will also fail to fully reach our goals. With good design, knowledge of the community, and full participation of the people, we will succeed. These are the lessons to be drawn from *Neighbors and Neighborhoods: Elements of Successful Community Design*.

The former governor of Maryland, Parris N. Glendening is president of Smart Growth America's Leadership Institute and the Governor's Institute on Community Design.

A NOTE TO THE READER

Large-scale developers are realizing that it's not enough to build a plain subdivision any more. They must also manufacture community itself, which has become an amenity people crave, right along with tray ceilings.

—Stephanie McCrummen[1]

It is not uncommon for developers to promote the idea of community as part of a housing package, and architects and planners write about collaborative communities, gated communities, and the architecture of community.[2] They focus on specialized designs of houses and neighborhoods, clearly implying that good design can generate a sense of community. The evidence that physical design produces community seems to be based more on faith and wishful thinking than on serious research. The premise is not invalid, but it raises a number of questions, especially for me, about the role of design in residential communities. Is there a link between the kind of neighborhood that people live in and their tendency to come together as a community? And if there is, what are the active elements of such a neighborhood, and how do they function?

I began thinking about residential communities in the mid-1990s, when I was working with Ralph Taylor, professor of criminal justice at Temple University, on a study that involved interviews with neighborhood leaders in 58 Baltimore neighborhoods.[3] We asked about local organizations and issues that brought neighborhood residents together. Mary Hyde—who also worked with us on the study and used the data for her PhD dissertation, which compared the concept of sense of community with that of attachment to place—introduced me to the extensive social science literature on community.

Newspaper advertisement from *Baltimore Sun*, May 23, 2010, real estate section, 3

Figure N.1. *"In historical utopias, community was an intentional goal shared by individuals with allegiances to commonly held beliefs. In today's planned development, community is mostly a marketing term, aimed at a consumer niche to be attracted and recruited through effective advertising"* (Ross, Celebration Chronicles, 238).

I knew generally what planners and architects wrote on the subject, but much of what sociologists, psychologists, anthropologists, and geographers said was new to me. I found their ideas stimulating and enlightening, but their definitions of community did not fit the descriptions that we were hearing in our Baltimore interviews. And so I began to explore the connection between housing and community for myself.

This book is a record of my exploration. The journey led me into questions about scientific methods and artistic principles, what we know and what we believe to be true, and accepted and applied meanings of the words *design* and *designer*. I discovered that the neighborhood–community connection is more real than scientists tend to believe and less direct than designers tend to think it is. I invite the reader to join me on the journey.

ACKNOWLEDGMENTS

I have drawn on the work of teachers, researchers, and designers. Kevin Lynch taught me that the purpose of design is to benefit people, not places; Ralph Taylor helped me to understand the value of rigorous research; Melvin Levin showed me that one must look to the past in order to understand the present; and I have benefited from the research and critiques of my students at the University of Maryland. Some ideas in this book had a trial run at conferences of the Environmental Design Research Association and the International Association for People-Environment Studies. Jack Nasar provided thoughtful comments on an early draft. If the language and structure of the book are clear, it is thanks in large measure to George F. Thompson and to understanding and careful editors at the Center for American Places and APA Planners Press. I am grateful to the School of Architecture, Planning, and Preservation at the University of Maryland for its financial assistance. And I am grateful to the residents of Baltimore and Columbia, Maryland, who agreed to be interviewed, were generous with their time, and answered my questions with good grace.

INTRODUCTION

Neighbors & Neighborhoods

—It's a close-knit community. Everybody is "family," everybody knows everybody.

—It's good to know you are not alone here.
—Residents of Locust Point, Baltimore[1]

There are more than 300 neighborhoods in the city of Baltimore, each a discrete geographic area with its own name. One neighborhood is called Locust Point. Its approximately 1,100 modest row houses are located on a peninsula that juts into the Baltimore harbor, dividing the Middle Branch of the Patapsco River from the Northwest Harbor and extending from Federal Hill to Fort McHenry. The houses sit in the shadow of what was once a huge grain elevator (since converted to condominiums), surrounded by railroads and hemmed in by industries and shipping yards.

A neighborhood is always a physical place, and so the neighborhood of Locust Point can be described by its surroundings, which consist of a cluster of row houses, a school, a park, several churches, and a number of bars and restaurants. But Locust Point is more than geography and buildings. It is also

Figure I.1. *This aerial view of Baltimore shows Fort McHenry on the right and Federal Hill on the left. Locust Point is in the center, a cluster of buildings surrounded by railroad lines. The picture shows the neighborhood, not the community. They are not the same.*

a community: a group of people who have similar interests, know one another, look out for one another, belong to the same organizations, and support the same establishments. This became clear in interviews with 54 residents conducted by students in the Urban Studies and Planning Program at the University of Maryland. The quotations in this chapter, unless otherwise identified, are excerpted from those interviews.[2]

Irish, German, and Polish immigrants settled Locust Point. After their boats docked at the foot of Andre Street, the newcomers disembarked and registered at the local immigration office. Many found employment at the railroad yards and the port, set up house in the area, and never left. A Locust Point resident characterized the settlers as "hardworking men who worked in factories and married sweet women."

They had similar jobs, and so they "knew everybody and could relate."

Many of their descendants still live in the neighborhood, often in the houses in which they were born. Jim Neill, a local historian, quotes a resident who described her attitude as "born on Decatur Street, die on Decatur Street," which is typical of Locust Pointers, as locals are known. Over the years, many families have intermarried and remained in the area, meaning several generations live within a few blocks. Newcomers are warned: "Don't talk about anybody, 'cause they're all related." A resident, discussing a house fire in Locust Point that had happened recently before his interview, said, "There's so much family down here—the first thing you think is whether you know them."[3] Even Locust Pointers who are not related share similar values—which one resident identified as home, family, faith, and beer—and have known one another for a long time. They do not always agree on every issue, but they get along because of their common interests.

Residents care for one another, saying, "If someone needs help, somebody will be there to help them," and "If you stumble here, somebody will be there to pick you up." They socialize in the local bars and congregate in the park. A group of men, who are known as the Supreme Court, can be seen every day on the same park bench. One resident described sitting out on the front steps:

> In the summertime people go out, and Lyn's got a little bench there, and we'll sit on the bench and it's like, you know, Marvin'll come out, Lyn will come out, lady down the street that's widowed, she'll come out, Miss Mary, Mr. Jim, and everyone will come out, and we'll just be like sitting on our steps talking, and it could be like four or five families, and not talking about anything really, but just sitting out.

Because so many residents have grown up in the neighborhood, it is common for locals to refer to married women by their maiden names and to call places by the names they had when they were growing up; people who are new to the area find it difficult to understand this shared community history. In their conversations, residents make frequent references to the past, and childhood stories are passed down from one generation to the next.

Locust Pointers substantially agree on how to define the physical boundaries of the neighborhood: On three sides it is bounded by industrial land and water, and on the fourth side, where "the Point" meets "the Hill" (Federal Hill), residents draw an imaginary boundary line down the center of Lawrence Street. One resident remembers that as a young girl, she could not bring a boyfriend from "up the Hill" back to Locust Point, because the Locust Point boys would have beaten him up.

At one time, Locust Pointers could find everything they needed without leaving the neighborhood. Older residents remember when there was a bake store, a dry-goods store, a grocery store, or a mom-and-pop store on every corner. Today, most of the small stores have closed, run out of business by chain supermarkets. There is an elementary school, a park, a recreation center, several restaurants, 18 bars, and on the neighborhood's border with Federal Hill, a small shopping center. There are three churches—Lutheran, Episcopal, and Catholic—whose congregations work together for the benefit of the entire community. (A new pastor was told, "Don't schedule anything without checking with the other churches.") There are a number of clubs, including the Honeymoon Pleasure Club (a social and fraternal organization), That Old Gang of Mine Club (for men), the Belles Club (for women), the local branch of the Knights of Columbus, and several senior-citizens clubs that meet at the neighborhood recreation center. The churches and the clubs host regular dinners, and Locust Pointers say you can attend one of these dinners every night of the week.

With approximately 200 members, the Locust Point Civic Association (LPCA) is the largest community organization in the area. The LPCA has committed leadership and excellent political connections, and it represents all of the residents, although "there are just some who won't put forth the effort unless it is a problem that involves them personally."[4] The LPCA keeps residents informed, steps in when residents neglect their properties, and acts as an intermediary in dealing with outside organizations and agencies. A resident described it as the community's "conduit for one voice."

Alain Jaramillo

Figure I.2. *The annual Locust Point Festival is the Locust Point Civic Association's major fund-raiser. Residents say that they work for days in advance to prepare food in the church kitchens for the highly anticipated event. The association uses the proceeds from the event to "put on holiday things for kids," in the words of one resident, and make improvements in the community, such as helping to install air-conditioning and repair the roof in the recreation center.*

In recent years, Locust Point has been changing. Many of the old industrial plants have closed. Many of the younger people work outside the area and, despite their family ties, leave Locust Point in search of better housing and schools. As a result, Locust Point has a relatively high proportion of elderly people and families with small children. Meanwhile, young, white-collar professionals are attracted to Locust Point. They live in new apartments or town houses and work in the revitalized industrial buildings along the waterfront and Fort Avenue, a street whose uses now include high-tech firms, an architect's office, a coffee shop, a wine bar, and a health club. Some are buying and renovating row houses. Longtime residents view these "brass-lampers" (a resident's term for the newcomers) with suspicion and "watch new people tooth and nail" to make sure they are "all right." The general feeling among established Locust Pointers is that the newcomers are less community oriented, interested in looking out only for themselves. Some locals say newcomers do not patronize the local facilities or attend community functions unless they "have their toes stepped on." Many longtime residents fear that the newcomers will erode the close-knit nature of Locust Point, causing the atmosphere of community to ultimately disappear. Ironically, new residents see the strong sense of community as one of the main attractions of the area.

I begin this book with a description of Locust Point as an example of a real-life Mayberry—the kind of place many social scientists must have in mind when they think about the concept of community.[5] See, for example, these selected definitions of *community*:

- An association among people characterized by a high level of interdependency and close emotional ties, in which people are "held together by shared understandings and a sense of obligation"[6]
- A representation of "something in the human condition that eternally yearns for a greater sense of connectedness, yearns to reach out and deeply touch others, throwing off the pain and loneliness of separation to experience unity with others"[7]
- "The smallest territorial group that can embrace all aspects of social life . . . the smallest local group that can be a complete society"[8]
- "The policy-deciding, self- or identity-maintaining social system of families residing in a particular area which confronts collectively problems arising from the sharing of the area"[9]
- "That combination of social units and systems which perform the major social functions having locality reference"[10]
- "A network of interpersonal relationships and emotional investments"[11]
- "The place where I'm known, where I'm safe to be known, for better or worse, on many levels"[12]

The truth is, however, that most neighborhoods are not like Locust Point, and these definitions do not apply to them.

Interviews with leaders in 58 community organizations in other Baltimore neighborhoods show that residential communities tend to be loose associations whose members have a narrow range of interests, and relationships among residents are changeable, tentative, and superficial.[13] Actions such as people waving to one another in the street, chatting over the garden fence, borrowing a cup of sugar, and attending an occasional community meeting do not necessarily translate into an invitation to dinner or a sense of loss if a neighbor moves away.

This raises questions about the nature of community: the importance of community, the relationship between a neighborhood and a community, and the motivation for residents to form a community.

Locust Point also shows that residents can form a community without help from a designer—a fact that is easily forgotten when planners and architects present themselves as critical actors in the process of creating communities. A recent Planners Book Service Catalog, published by the American Planning Association (whose motto is "Making Great Communities Happen"), lists 24 books about neighborhood design that have the word *community* in their titles. Examples include *Aesthetics, Community Character and the Law; Parking Handbook for Small Communities;* and *Is Your Community a Great Place to Live?* Architects remark that "excellent architecture has the potential to build community" and "New Urbanism . . . represents a rediscovery of architectural and planning traditions that have shaped some of the most livable, memorable communities in America."[14]

If designers make excessive claims that they are essential for the creation of community, social scientists err in the other direction. They recognize that the form and appearance of the physical environment can affect social behavior, yet they tend to see the elements—buildings and spaces—as givens to be observed, used, and rated, but not shaped. If, for example, they associate community with density, they do not consider the way building layout and the location of building entrances can mitigate or intensify the way density is experienced; if they associate community with physical boundaries, they do not consider what elements or arrangements make effective boundaries. By ignoring the creative-artistic aspects of the physical environment, social scientists imply—and some assert—that designers should content themselves with the provision of adequate facilities and leave the matter of creating community to others.[15]

This raises questions about the role of design in creating communities: Can the qualities that evolved organically in Locust Point be introduced through design; if they can, have they been; and if so, where and how?

The qualities that contribute to Locust Point as a community include both physical and social components. Community resides not only in the presence of churches, bars, restaurants, a park, and a recreation center but also in the continuing presence of residents who are familiar with local history, conform to local customs, are represented by an active community organization, and have similar values and lifestyles. As these are components of community, they should all be concerns for community designers.

This raises questions about the nature of community design: What is its scope, who are the designers, what should their goals be, and how do we measure their achievements?

I use the three sets of questions raised by Locust Point as a framework for this book. Part 1 is about the nature of community. I turn to the social sciences to find out what research has taught us about the condition of community, kinds of communities, and community-generating properties of neighborhoods. Part 2 is about the role of design in creating communities. I look at the histories of planned communities to find what community-generating properties are incorporated in their designs and what forms they take. Part 3 is about the nature of community design. I synthesize what I have learned from research and design about the principles, goals, and process of community design. I conclude that a design can incorporate the elements that create a community as well as those that support and sustain it.

In all, I hope to address the questions posed by James Rouse in a speech at the University of California, Berkeley, in 1963: What is the purpose of a community? What constitutes a successful community? What are the tests, guideposts, or comparisons by which we could measure the success of one community against another, and how do we create "communities in which people feel important and uplifted"?[16]

It is necessary to explain some of the key terms used in the book because they are open to different interpretations. I use the word *community* to refer to a set of social relationships, and *neighborhood* to refer to a physical place. Jonathan Barnett reverses the two meanings—for him, a community is a physical entity, and a neighborhood is a network of "people who know each other, share some of their social life, help each other out in emergencies, and get together to manage community projects"—while Henry Sanoff uses *community* to mean the active participation of community members in the design process.[17] I use the word *design* to refer not exclusively (or even necessarily) to the actions of urban designers, architects, and landscape architects but also to actions by developers, promoters, leasing agents, image makers, organizers, and residents themselves. Some argue that community design is about "the physical shelter of human settlements" and that my approach involves "raids into the domains of social institutions and of mental life" and so is outside the scope of design.[18] But as I see it, the purpose of community design is to create relationships between people, not buildings, and the ultimate measure of a community design must be the extent to which it brings people together.

PART 1

Social Science Research

CHAPTER 1

What Is Community?

In Ersilia, to establish the relationships that sustain the city's life, the inhabitants stretch strings from the corners of the houses, white or black or gray or black-and-white according to whether they mark a relationship of blood, of trade, authority, agency. When the strings become so numerous that you can no longer pass among them, the inhabitants leave: the houses are dismantled; only the strings and their supports remain.

—Italo Calvino[1]

A community is a particular type of association, distinguishable from other forms of association such as cliques, gangs, action sets, and factions.[2] George Hillery, in an oft-quoted paper published in 1955, looks at 94 definitions of community (he uncovers many more) in the sociological literature of the first half of the 20th century. All but three of the 94 studies agree that community means people in social interaction; 24 agree that it also means people having common ends, norms, and means; and 55 agree that it also means people living in the same area.[3] In other words, most definitions of community include social interaction, common ties, and coresidency.

Psychologists believe that community-relevant behavior is motivated by a "sense of community." Seymour Sarason's *The Psychological Sense of Community* stimulated a decade and a half of lively scholarship that produced our current understanding of the term as meaning a feeling of "we-ness"; of belonging to a group whose members share a common destiny; being bound together by emotional ties rather than individual self-interest.[4] It is a feeling that each member is concerned about the welfare of the others.[5] In a seminal paper, David McMillan and David Chavis defined it as the feeling that one belongs to and identifies with a group, is accepted as a member, and is prepared to put the group's collective good before individual interests; that one can influence what the group does but is prepared to yield to group pressures; that one's needs will be met through membership of the group and through members' commitment to help one another; and that members have common experiences and a common history that add meaning to shared activities and shared surroundings.[6]

Sense of community is the motivation for people to behave in community-relevant ways. Neighborhood studies show people who express a stronger sense of community are more likely to engage in neighborly acts, express willingness to cooperate, participate in community organizations and in local affairs, make physical improvements, fight crime, support public school taxes, and operate social programs.[7]

People who have a stronger sense of community are also more likely to express feelings of satisfaction with life in their neighborhood and are more likely to think of their neighborhood as a community.[8] They are also inclined to identify neighbors by name, have friends and relatives living nearby, be longtime residents, and expect to stay there for a number of years.[9] Home owners who expect to continue living in the neighborhood for a number of years have also been found to have a stronger sense of community. A sense of community depends in large measure on community attachment, or the number of friends and acquaintances in the neighborhood, which tends to increase the longer one lives in an area.

Studies have found that certain people are more likely to have a sense of community than others. They include those who have what Stephanie Riger and Paul Lavrakis call "behavioral rootedness," people who lead active family lives, married couples and couples with children, people who have friends and relatives in the neighborhood, longtime residents, and individuals who are emotionally stable.[10] Older residents tend to have a greater sense of community than younger ones. Those who are fearful of crime have less sense of community than those who feel safe.[11] People express their sense of community in different ways: Women interact with more of their neighbors than men do (although these interactions are not necessarily more frequent or more intimate), and people with higher education and income typically know and engage with more of their neighbors, but they rely on them less for friendship and support.[12]

Following George Hillery's findings, I will consider a group of people to be a community if its members interact in a way that reflects shared interests. If, in addition, they live in the same area, I will refer to the area as a neighborhood.[13] In this book I am concerned with neighborhood-based (that is, residential) communities.

Alain Jaramillo

Figure 1.1. *Every summer, the* Afro-American *newspaper organizes a Clean Block Competition in Baltimore and awards prizes for the best-looking street blocks. The improvements in the blocks reflect residents' coordinated efforts. This photo was taken in the Upton neighborhood in 1978.*

I use the word *neighborhood* in its most general sense, to mean the geographic area that residents perceive as an extension of their home. A neighborhood-based community is a particular form of community. It is a group of people bound together by interests that stem directly from the condition of being residents of the same neighborhood; these are interests they share only with coresidents and only as long as they remain coresidents. I characterize these interests as: all in the same place; all in the same boat; all of the same kind; one for all; and all in the family.

1. All in the Same Place

    Coresidents are drawn to the physical form and appearance of the neighborhood and to the local amenities that it offers. Think of neighborhoods that are distinctive, with memorable buildings and good services.

2. All in the Same Boat

    Coresidents, as a group, stand to gain or lose from the actions of individual residents, and individuals stand to gain or lose from the actions of the group. Think of neighborhood improvements that increase the value of an individual property, or of a street that becomes less desirable because a neighbor allows his property to deteriorate.

3. All of the Same Kind

    Coresidents are drawn together because they share the same status, values, and practices. Think of neighborhoods that reflect a racial, ethnic, or class identity.

4. One for All

    Coresidents are drawn together by their membership in an organization that represents and advocates for their common interests, and also speaks for them with a single voice. Think of residents who attend neighborhood meetings, serve on committees, vote in elections, and pay membership dues.

5. All in the Family

    Coresidents are drawn together by shared memories and local customs and rituals. Think of neighborhoods in which meaningful buildings are preserved and protected, and where people retell the same stories and repeat the same annual festivals.

Neighborhood-based communities, like other communities, do not come about naturally; they are deliberately constructed in order to further common interests. We used to believe that people who share the same values and interests are predisposed to interact and cooperate with one another, and therefore gravitate to the same part of the city.[14] We thought that community and neighborhood are two sides of the same coin. But this ignored the fact that coresidency is the result of choice for some, and lack of choice for others.

Architects and urban planners see loss of community as the consequence of poor neighborhood design. They say that neighborhoods do not look like or have the feel of community: Densities are low, there are few pedestrian-friendly places, there is little chance for people to meet casually and spontaneously, and residents lose the spirit of cooperation and the interpersonal skills necessary for negotiating differences. They become mistrustful of one another and participate less in formal and informal associations. They do not identify with their neighborhoods and do not feel affection for or take pride in them. Unhappy and frustrated, they yearn for old-time small towns with their pedestrian-oriented streets, small-scale, walk-to stores and workplaces, convenient public transportation, active public areas, and local institutions.[15]

Social science researchers also see community through the lens of their own particular discipline. Anthropologists and biologists say humans are social animals who have developed and prevailed precisely because of our ability to work together for the common good. We form communities because it is human nature to do so.[16] Aristotle writes that it is only through interaction in communities that we are able to acquire and practice the good habits that make it possible for us to be truly happy.[17]

Psychologists say it is in communities that we develop the self-esteem, competence, and control that we need for our individual well-being. When we are deprived of community, we feel unwanted and rejected, becoming easy prey to mental illness and other psychological disturbances; we become unhappy, lonely, anxious, frustrated, and alienated, even psychopathic. Life loses meaning and becomes empty.[18]

Sociologists think community is the medium through which we learn about social responsibility, friendship, love, status and role, order and disorder, and guilt and innocence. A community allows us to pass information from one generation to

another, socialize children, acculturate newcomers, accommodate group differences, and build a common culture.[19]

Political scientists say communities bring people together to
discuss common needs, values, and problems, and to express
and advocate for common interests. Through community we
build networks, norms, and trust; and we create an atmosphere
of civic responsibility, informal social control, neighborly
goodwill, and mutual concern for the common good. Without
communities to mediate between our private and public lives,
society and democracy would not exist.[20]

There is agreement that community is important to us, both
as individuals and as members of society. But many feel that
we in the United States have become less community minded
than in the past.[21]

Bellah and others, in *Habits of the Heart*, blame this lack of
community on the nature of our society, which values individual rights and freedoms over the well-being of the collective.
We do not measure people's success by their contribution to
public life but rather by their personal incomes and lifestyles,
the quality of their homes, and the prestige of the areas in
which they live. We do not require that people participate in
community affairs. Those who become involved see it as an
investment rather than a duty, and so they choose communities
of similar-minded people, ensuring that their membership will
bring them the greatest personal rewards.[22]

Other researchers blame the loss of community on the
changing role of local organizations in civic life. They argue
that in the past, primary groups such as family, neighborhood,
and church played an important role in people's lives and in
society as a whole; these groups had a great deal of autonomy,
and people participated in order to gain status, security, and
identity. Today, many primary groups have dissolved, and others have been replaced by large, impersonal institutions, which
cut across local boundaries and are guided by outside policies and decisions. These groups are devoted to single-issue
causes and do not instill in their members a shared sense of the
larger society.[23]

Still others believe television and Internet use contribute to
the general weakening of community ties by making it possible for individuals to live farther apart, replacing face-to-face

interactions, gatherings, and informal conversations with superficial contacts. Similarly, telecommuting weakens people's connection to their work community.[24]

Another factor to consider as a reason for a reduced sense of community is a high crime rate. Crime in a neighborhood makes residents feel threatened, causing them to avoid their neighbors, go places in the neighborhood by car instead of walking, and stay away from public areas.[25]

There are researchers who ascribe the loss of community to changes in work patterns and modes of communication. They argue that as automobile, telephone, and Internet usage goes up, workplaces become more scattered and housing choices increase, so that fewer people work in the neighborhood in which they live, and fewer yet live near friends and family. At the same time, households have become smaller, and more women have taken outside jobs. The overall result has been that people spend less time at home; they feel less attached and committed to their neighborhoods, make smaller investments in their local communities, and are inclined to move more often. Using cars rather than walking around the neighborhood reduces residents' chances of forming social ties. In many instances, when residents disagree with one another they avoid direct contact and rely instead on intermediaries such as the police, a management company, or a local residents association to resolve a dispute.[26]

Because residents are able to interact with people in all parts of the city, local communities can transcend the neighborhood or represent part of a neighborhood; and they can be nested within or overlap other communities.[27]

A leader of the community association representing the Washington Village/Pigtown neighborhood in Baltimore illustrates how complex the relationships are between social and geographic areas, and how perceptions of neighborhood and community boundaries are constantly being revised and redefined.[28] Here is an excerpt from his interview narrative:

> The interviewee explained that there are three community organizations in his neighborhood: Southwest Community Council, Hearts of Pigtown, and the Washington Village Improvement Association . . . In general, the three organizations are quite

feudal. The Hearts of Pigtown represents the "old guard" of the poor and less educated residents who have broken off and are not accepting any new members. The Washington Village Improvement Association has been taken over by the newer, more educated, upper-class residents. Recently, the presidents of the three associations . . . got together and tried to help the associations to get along. This effort failed and the associations all lost members.[29]

Another community leader was asked to map the boundaries of the communities and social groups in the same part of the city.[30] His maps show multiple communities coexisting within the same neighborhood.

Community leaders agree that different communities may serve different populations within a single area and that social boundaries may change over time while geographic boundaries do not:

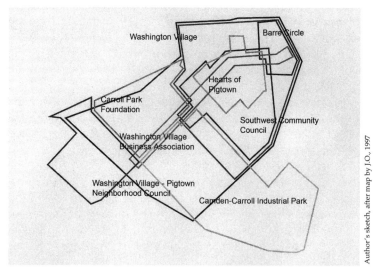

Figure 1.2. *A community leader in the Pigtown neighborhood, in Baltimore, was asked to draw the boundaries of organizations in his area. His map shows that a resident may fall within the boundaries of a number of different communities all at the same time.*

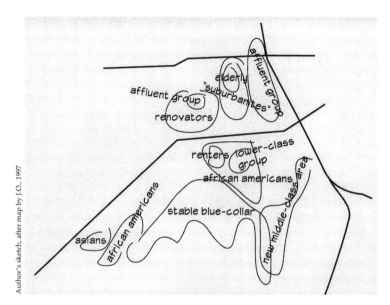

Figure 1.3. *The same community leader who drew Figure 1.2 was asked to map the location of social groups living in the Pigtown neighborhood. His map shows that informal social areas underlie and cut across the areas claimed by formal community organizations.*

In 1979, there was a division between Canton and West Canton. West Canton may have been created because people in the area thought they were being "ill-served" . . . Most of the residents in the area simply call it Canton . . . There are several areas with different names, including Tindeco, . . . Canton Square, . . . Canton Cove, and the Anchorage Towers . . . Another group, called Concerned Citizens to Save Our Community, is also active in the community . . . The Canton Highlandtown Community Association represents about half of the residents in the area.[31]

Hollins Hill is one neighborhood among three that are represented by the Roundhouse Coalition. In 1970, Hollins Park had a small community organization headed by a little old lady, A. G. . . . A. G. convinced Hollins Hills Community Organization

Author's sketch, after map by J.O., 1997

to merge with Hollins Park Community Association so that they would have more political clout . . . The new merged community organization decided to represent Little Lithuania . . . Then, in the 1980s, the community became involved in the Poppleton Urban Renewal program, where they stopped calling their organization Hollins Park Community Association . . . In the late 1980s . . . the Roundhouse Neighborhood Coalition came along, where "the same players, but with different uniforms" formed the new neighborhood association.[32]

The association is discussing whether to extend the boundaries to the west across Harford Road because there are more problems occurring in that area that need to be addressed. The interviewer . . . explained that the area behind 25th Street that used to contain the Mayflower warehouse, an area basically used as a dumping ground . . . was added to the neighborhood boundaries between 1980 and 1990.[33]

Residents talk about changing their membership from one community to another while continuing to live at the same address. The following excerpt is from an interview in 2001:

When the girls were little . . . they both went to the elementary school . . . For us, in that moment of time . . . the elementary school and the neighborhood center were very important to us . . . The girls got older and they went to middle school. And suddenly . . . the middle school and high school became very important . . . So that became our world. And then the kids went off to college, and suddenly the neighborhood center and the village center didn't mean anything . . . Our world became extended up to Syracuse . . . As we became empty nesters, suddenly other things were of interest to us . . . Some of our friends would move from the single-family houses to [a different village], or they would move to larger houses in [another, more distant] village. So suddenly our . . . friendship patterns were expanded.[34]

Neighborhood structure remains important: Neighbors will always be the most convenient people to call on for favors such as exchanging tools or sugar, taking in the mail, and keeping an eye on one's house; and even if one does not associate with coresidents often, just seeing familiar faces gives a feeling of belonging and of membership.[35] Yet neighborhood-based communities in general have changed in significant ways: Many have become single-interest groups whose members come together only when something threatens the quality and value of their homes. Relationships with neighbors do not necessarily require frequent or intense interaction.[36]

There are, however, certain neighborhood characteristics that help to bring residents together as a community. Research suggests that these are homogeneity, community organization, suitable physical settings and facilities, and ongoing traditions. I will discuss each of these in turn.

Similarity, or like-mindedness, is perhaps the most important contributor to community. It refers to people having a similar level of income (especially if they have higher income), education (especially if they are well educated), and socioeconomic status.[37] It is associated with shared ideology, ethnicity, race, tenure, degree of urbanization, and stage in the life cycle.[38] Similar people tend to speak the same language (literally and figuratively), which makes it easier to communicate: Many things can be implied with little or no explanation, and many actions can be anticipated and are less likely to be misinterpreted. Better communication makes living together less stressful and interaction more likely.

Like-minded people do not necessarily agree with one another on every issue, but they know how to get along, and they tend to express a high degree of conformity. Weiss says like-minded people live their private lives in much the same way, dress alike, buy the same products, read the same newspapers, belong to the same political party, spend their leisure time doing the same things, have similar locational preferences, and live in similar houses.[39]

Assembling a body of similar and like-minded residents is the single most powerful way to generate a sense of community, but there is also the danger that it may breed parochial attitudes and further social segregation.[40] This concern has given rise to public programs that support the creation of mixed income neighborhoods, but there is a question as to whether the mix is sustainable and whether the residents really become a community (see chapter 7 for more discussion about these issues). A resident of Columbia, Maryland, told me, "It doesn't mean that we can't get along with different socioeconomic class people. Actually, I know and like a lot of them. It's just that we don't make connections to form a lasting bond, I guess."[41]

Community organizations are another element that, research shows, strengthens sense of community. These organizations provide a vehicle for individuals to relate to one another as they work through issues of belonging, shared interests, and discordant agendas. They represent individual interests to the larger community and promote the belief that the individual is part of a larger whole. It becomes possible for individuals to affect community events by actively engaging with one another, and this creates a sense of interdependence among residents. Some community organizations emerge as a byproduct of participation in a planning process (see chapter 7).

Successful community organizations are characterized by commitment, vision, the ability to articulate needs, the existence of procedures to resolve conflict, open channels of communication, a system for decision making, and a way of managing relations with the larger society.[42] Community organizations give people a pretext for meeting one another without having to commit to developing friendships. They transform private individuals into members of a community.[43]

The physical setting also contributes to community. Boundaries—such as main roads, bodies of water, and open spaces—can be useful starting points for residents who want to create a community. They make it easier to define the jurisdiction of a neighborhood organization, represent the community to outside groups, and defend the area against threats from outside.[44]

Local facilities contribute to the formation of community, and residential use of such facilities and services can serve as a measure of social cohesion.[45] People who use the same schools, convenience stores, parks, playgrounds, and religious, cultural, and civic institutions develop a common interest in the adequacy and level of service of the facilities, encouraging feelings of goodwill and the development of interpersonal relationships.[46] Residents who use the facilities can meet other members of the community. This is especially important for people who work in their homes and who have the impetus to get out for short periods of time and be around other people.[47]

Public spaces can be designed in such a way that people will use them for recreation, spend more time there, engage in a wide range of activities, and develop mutual interests centered around a common area.[48] People who meet by chance are more likely to interact if they are at leisure, because they have more time to socialize than if they were at work or attending to chores. Leisure activities tend to be seen as play, and play evokes a sense of camaraderie.[49] People are more likely to interact in a meaningful way in a play setting than in a work setting—for instance, in a park rather than in a store. Of course, families with little leisure time are less likely to interact with their neighbors, no matter what facilities are available. Shared facilities raise questions of responsibility for their maintenance and supervision; in the absence of an effective social mechanism to manage them, the interaction that they generate may be negative, leading to conflict, not friendship.[50]

Certain arrangements of houses, the provision and placement of shared facilities, the relative position of entrances, and the location of mailboxes, fences, access paths, parking lots, and playgrounds affect neighbor-to-neighbor interactions.[51] For example, residents on a cul-de-sac were found to have a greater sense of community and were more familiar with their neighbors than residents on through streets, and residents who lived on streets with a low volume of traffic were found to be more likely to engage in neighborly acts.[52]

As density increases, so does the likelihood of social contact. Higher density increases the need for residents to be considerate of their neighbors and to negotiate disagreements when they arise; and when their neighbors are different from themselves, to be tolerant of these differences. It also increases the value of common norms of behavior.[53] On the other hand, Anthony Wallace, in an early study conducted for the Philadelphia Housing Authority, points out that private yards in low-density areas can generate neighborly interaction.

> Each man maintains more or less regular, if informal, connection with his six or eight closest neighbors. The nexus is a common interest in property, lawn care, cement and carpentry work, maintenance and repair of power mowers, etc. He sees his neighbors and his neighbors see him, working or not

Courtesy of Kentlands and Duany Plater-Zyberk & Company

Figure 1.4. *Kentlands, a planned community in Maryland, requires fences in the belief that they encourage interaction with neighbors and passersby; Columbia, Maryland, on the other hand, disallows fences in the belief that they are unfriendly and discourage interaction.*

working. From time to time he lends or borrows tools. He shares a bottle of beer occasionally with two or three others. By criticism and praise of absent neighbors' efforts, standards of house appearance and facilities are established and disseminated. And matters of public concern are discussed in equally casual but effective fashion. *All of this depends upon the existence of a yard* [emphasis in the original].[54]

Chris Webster, looking at the neighborhood from his perspective as an economic geographer, sees it as a unit of collective consumption and production similar to a firm or a club. He writes that the "dependence of a household's welfare on the actions of others in the neighborhood suggests that an efficient allocation of property rights would require all property-owners in the street to have a claim on the value of every other property."[55] Duncan and Duncan, in their study of Bedford, New York, note that individual property owners benefit from large-lot zoning, even though this means that they cannot subdivide their property, because "the town as a whole retains a pastoral landscape that maintains high property values."[56]

Research also suggests that the nature of a community varies with its size—the size of the area over which it has jurisdiction, and the size of its membership. Gerald Suttles, in *The Social Construction of Communities*, suggests four critical areas around which communities can develop.

The Face-Block: An area where people know one another mainly because they happen to live close by or use the same facilities.

The Defended Neighborhood: The smallest area that has a corporate identity, a name that is recognized by members and outsiders, and facilities that residents use and share in the course of their daily lives.

The Community of Limited Liability: An officially recognized area with a name and official boundaries; it may contain several overlapping communities, some broad in scope and others focusing on a single issue, and people may choose to belong to one or more of them.[57]

The Expanded Community of Limited Liability: A large area of the city within which community groups get together in order to marshal large constituencies and gain political clout.

There are three critical ranges of membership size.[58] The smallest membership population is identified as 80 to 100 adults. A community of this size is able to fulfill the need for companionship to the fullest and ensure both variety of contacts and constancy of relationships. Even at this size, it is difficult to keep track of each individual's separate views and social activities, and so people reduce the effective number of fellow members by classifying them into subgroups and developing stereotypes for each group, or by relating to fellow members through the medium of a leader.[59]

The next critical membership ranges in size from 400 to 1,500 people, with an approximate ideal of 500. According to Gordon Taylor, this is "the largest group in which every individual can form some personal estimate of the significance of a majority of the other members of the group in relation to himself," yet it is still small enough so that members can associate with one another on a regular basis, provide mutual aid, and have open and trusting social relations. Hans Blumenfeld states that with 400 to 800 people, it is still possible for everybody to know everybody else by face, voice, and name; Terence Lee claims people think of their "social acquaintance area" as containing as many as 1,200 people, with an average of fewer than 1,000; and C. A. Doxiades says 1,500 people is the maximum size for a large neighborhood.[60]

The Israeli kibbutzim average 400 people, and the average size of successful communes in America during the 19th century was fewer than 500 people. These include the Hutterite colonies, with an average of about 100 people each; the Oneida Community, with 150 to 200 people; the Amana community, which was divided into villages that ranged in size from 150 to about 600 people; the Zoar community, with 500 people at its height; and the Rappite community, with 800 people at its largest. Shaker communities never numbered more than 600 people and were divided into "families" of 30 to 100 people.[61]

The third critical membership size is approximately 5,000 adults, with a range of 4,000 to 10,000 people. This is the number of people needed to support the provision of basic services. Cities before the Christian era contained between 5,000 and 10,000 people; larger cities of the medieval period were divided into quarters or precincts of not more than 10,000 people. The Baltimore neighborhood survey, referred to earlier, found a median size of 5,000 to 6,000 people in each neighborhood.[62]

Another powerful contributor to the building of a community is the presence of shared traditions. Traditions rooted in local places and events remind individuals of the original purposes and nature of their association, and they give communities a sense of continuity and direction in changing times.[63]

The physical setting can strengthen these traditions by triggering shared recollections of events that are known to (or were said to) have happened there. Community organizations help to retain the potency of traditions by documenting, inventing, retelling, and celebrating them through rituals, ceremonies, and festivals.[64] Over time, the celebrations themselves become part of the collective memory.

In a study that compared two small Italian towns, researchers found one town had a significantly higher sense of community than the other. The only notable difference was that the town put on an annual theatrical event involving about half of the local inhabitants, which demonstrates how a celebration can generate community.[65]

Residence in the same neighborhood does not, by itself, bring residents together as a community. As I have explained, neighborhoods are not necessarily coterminous with communities. However, some neighborhoods, such as Locust Point, are.[66] It is reasonable to argue that this is, at least in part, *because the neighborhood has community-generating properties*, or properties that reinforce community-relevant behavior. In part 2, I examine a number of planned communities to identify properties that can be community generating.[67] Each chapter focuses on a community property that is strongly supported by research. These properties are:

Homogeneity: The residents have shared values, aspirations, and goals, and recognize and conform to group norms.

Community Organizations: Neighborhood-based organizations create reasons and opportunities for residents to meet, and to work with one another on issues of local concern.

Suitable Physical Settings: The neighborhood accommodates and facilitates social interaction.

Ongoing Traditions: Residents have shared experiences, which are expressed in local traditions, stories, and celebrations.

My descriptions of the above properties are very general. They do not include all of the properties suggested by community research; and several properties, in various combinations and to varying degrees, may be present in any one design. The chapter divisions in part 2 serve as devices to identify properties that I believe both contribute to the formation of community and can be introduced through design.

I have several disclaimers regarding the selection of case histories in part 2. First, they consist exclusively or predominantly of houses rather than apartment buildings, which have their own design issues and deserve their own set of criteria. Also, I have restricted my choices to the United States. I have not included potentially valuable examples from Europe and elsewhere because I feel more comfortable discussing places whose background is familiar to me. (Having decided on this criterion, I deviate from it by including several early British examples because they have had a strong influence on community design in the United States.) In order to identify design elements that have been tested through repeated applications, I have chosen communities that, taken together, span a reasonably long period of time (about 130 years). Each of the communities I discuss has had an active, ongoing residents organization and, in addition, at least two of the general community-generating principles I list above. Finally, I have chosen communities that represent different degrees of resident interdependency, from those where members do little more than greet one another and perhaps offer to help in an emergency, to those where members are intimately involved with one another in their day-to-day lives.[68]

The development histories of these communities are selective accounts of actions and decisions that were intended (according to written statements) to contribute to the creation of community, or that I believe do so.[69] Much of my information for the development histories comes from secondary sources. I am aware that some of these sources may be incomplete, biased, or out of date; but I am only concerned that the information is true to its source, and that it illustrates design intentions. Because I am interested in the nature and effect of design decisions, and because later events may drastically change the relevance and effectiveness of these decisions, each history focuses on a period that is close to the point of design.

PART 2

Development Histories

CHAPTER 2

Homogeneity

The grouping of a number of families of much the same social
status, and with many tastes in common, has rendered possible at
Roland Park, as at other suburbs of like character, the development
of social life in a degree manifestly impossible under the conditions
prevailing in the average city neighborhood.

—Walden Fawcett[1]

The development histories of the four communities described
in this chapter (Roland Park, Maryland; Radburn, New Jersey;
Twin Oaks, Virginia; and Seaside, Florida) show the procedures each community incorporated to attract residents with
the same values, aspirations, and goals—people who were
likely to get along with one another. Roland Park did this by
marketing to people in the same socioeconomic class; Radburn
did it by excluding people who were felt to be incompatible;
the Twin Oaks Community instituted an elaborate interview
and trial process to ensure that all residents subscribe to a communitarian way of life; and Seaside created an image aimed at
people with traditional values.

The designs of Roland Park, Radburn, Twin Oaks, and
Seaside highlight the inherently discriminatory nature of communities: They embrace those who belong and exclude those
who do not. Some of the methods used in these designs have
since been ruled unconstitutional, but screening of one kind or
another is still widespread in communities. Think, for example, of realtors who steer clients away from certain areas and

into others; common-interest communities and condominium associations who set up committees to interview prospective residents; retirement communities that exclude those below a certain age; and most commonly, high-priced developments that screen prospective residents on the basis of their ability to pay. Like it or not, screening is purposeful and deliberate— that is, it is introduced by design, and it is done in the interest of creating community. One may question whether screening passes the test of ethical conduct. I touch again on this dilemma in chapter 7.

ROLAND PARK, BALTIMORE, MARYLAND, 1891

Roland Park, in Baltimore, sits on high ground approximately four miles north of the center city.[2] To the east, the land falls gently to Stony Run, and to the west, it breaks up in folds and drops steeply to Jones Falls. When the Roland Park Company acquired the property for the purpose of developing "a sub-urban town," it was outside the city limits, divided among several country estates. The developmental work was accom-plished in successive phases.

Edward Bouton, the company's secretary and general man-ager, was in charge of the project. George Kessler, a landscape architect based in Kansas City, Missouri, designed the first phase of the development. Kessler laid out a wide main road (Roland Avenue) along the spine of the hill, and residential lots to the east. The western part of the site was designed by Olm-sted, Olmsted, and Eliot (known later as the Olmsted Brothers after the death of Eliot), who created a network of winding roads that curve and branch, following the natural contours of the land, and edge into the sides of the hills. The roads are linked by stepped pedestrian paths to cul-de-sacs, which extend as spurs along the hilltops. Most lots were offered for single-family detached houses, but there were also scattered sites for clustered two-family houses and row houses, and for several apartment buildings.

Bouton intended to bring the "best people in Maryland" to Roland Park. To accomplish his goal, he opened a streetcar line providing direct public transport downtown and founded a country club. He built an elegant clubhouse on a grassy hillside with views down to the floor of the Jones Falls valley and appointed a board whose members—except for himself and William G. Nolting, one of the architects of the clubhouse— were all listed in Baltimore's social register. Bouton reasoned that if he brought this select group of people out to Roland Park for recreational and social reasons and exposed them to the joys of country life, he would tempt them to leave their homes in town and move to the suburbs "in order to turn to pleasurable account every spare moment of their time."[3]

Bouton's strategy succeeded. Roland Park was settled by upper-middle-class professionals, who were active in reform movements and committed to civic life. Racial and ethnic restrictions were not an issue in the early days because they were simply understood to be in place, but in later years, they were written into the title deeds.

Bouton introduced development controls (there was no land-use zoning at the time) because he believed that people who agree to these kinds of controls make congenial neighbors. The Roland Park Company set a minimum cost for all houses to be built and required that new residents sign a covenant that gave the company the right to review and approve all architectural designs and future changes. The company permitted a variety of design styles, ranging from classical to picturesque, but residents were required to employ an architect, use natural building materials, and set the home well back from the road.

Roland Park soon fostered an active social life. This was due in no small part to the fact that the residents were all members of the same social class. Because the new residents were city people and inexperienced at country living, the Roland Park Company put out a monthly magazine, the *Roland Park Review*, which, in addition to reporting local news, provided advice, hints, and admonitions to the residents on issues such as trash disposal, civil behavior, gardening, and dealing with cats, dogs, and wildlife.[4]

Bouton gave sites for free or at substantially reduced rates to churches and assisted in the formation of a private elementary school. He built a small shopping center (then called a "business block") at the terminus of the streetcar line on Roland Avenue. The business block housed a drugstore, grocery, bakery, and post office, and became a popular meeting place for residents. Bouton sparked the organization of the Woman's Club of Roland Park and provided members with a space to hold their meetings, teas, musicales, dances, whist parties, and lectures until 1902, when the club built its own headquarters on Roland Avenue.

He also pushed for the organization of the Roland Park Civic League to supplement the amenities provided by the company, which included a supply of piped freshwater ("as pure as could possibly be obtained"), scientific sewerage using glazed tile sewer pipes, and sidewalks that were paved and lined with shade trees.[5] Bouton wanted to provide "an educational, moral, social and beneficial association . . . for the promotion of friendly social intercourse . . . taking action from time to time . . . for the purpose of fostering the common good and welfare of the members."[6] One of the civic league's first actions was to form a volunteer fire company.

In 1909, as the Roland Park Company was phasing out its work in the area, Bouton set up the Roland Park Roads and Maintenance Corporation to assume the tasks of enforcing deed restrictions and maintaining the water mains, roads, lanes, and common land. He turned over the control and ownership of the corporation to the Roland Park Civic League, thus creating an informal, resident-run government supported by mandatory annual dues from each property owner.

From Roland Park's inception, Bouton lived there. Frederick Law Olmsted, Jr., wrote of Bouton: "He has been 'the whole thing' at Roland Park . . . daily successfully handling . . . the situation on the spot."[7] He oversaw the installation of the sewer and water supply systems, electric lines, streetcar tracks, roads, and paved sidewalks. Bouton also had a hand in the design of street signs and the selection of ornamental trees and shrubs.

More than a century after its founding, the area retains its charm and reputation as a desirable place in which to live. The racial and ethnic restrictions are no longer applicable, but the area remains predominantly upper-middle class. The Roland Park Civic League and the Roland Park Roads and Maintenance Corporation are still active, and have been joined by two other community-run organizations: the Roland Park Swimming Pool and the Roland Park Community Foundation.

Photo from Clarence Stein papers, #3600, courtesy of the Division of Rare Manuscript Collections, Cornell University Library

Figure 2.1. *The Roland Park Country School for Girls, in Baltimore, was established in 1894 with money loaned by the Roland Park Company. This photo was taken in 1931.*

RADBURN, NEW JERSEY, 1929

Clarence Stein and Henry Wright designed the planned neighborhood of Radburn, New Jersey, for the City Housing Corporation.[8] Their original goal was to create a town for a population of 25,000 to 30,000 people. Radburn was to be the first of a series of garden cities in the United States.[9] (The concept of the garden city, imported from England, is described in chapter 4.) The Great Depression halted construction efforts, however, and what was completed was essentially a small residential development with a population of approximately 3,000, which was embedded within a conventional-pattern suburb. The development occupies 149 acres. It consists of 674 units of single-family detached houses, town houses, duplexes, and apartments, along with a neighborhood retail center, elementary school, interdenominational church, parks, and recreation facilities.

In the original plans, the land was divided into blocks of 30 to 50 acres in size, each surrounded by roadways. Two of these blocks, taken together, would have made a neighborhood of 5,000 to 10,000 residents, each with its own elementary school, community center, and recreation center. Each neighborhood had a shopping center and a high school. The high school was located, symbolically, at the highest point of elevation. The school, which had an auditorium, a gymnasium, a library, and perhaps a small museum, was supposed to provide a place for residents to exchange ideas and interests. A large regional shopping center and an educational and cultural center served the whole town.

Stein and Wright designed simple buildings and included design restrictions in each purchase deed in order to ensure that residents could "not destroy the harmony or spoil the plan by building structures inappropriate in design and location."[10] The site layout was highly innovative in its own right. Each perimeter roadway provided access to cul-de-sac streets, which were 20 to 30 feet wide and penetrated, fingerlike, into the blocks. Each cul-de-sac provided access to 20 houses; the cul-de-sac served the kitchen side of the house, which was intended mainly as an entrance for goods and service deliveries. The front door was on the opposite, or living room, side and was connected by a pedestrian path to other houses and to a four- to six-acre interior-block park.[11]

The path system extended under or over the perimeter roadway and into the adjacent block, providing separate pedestrian access to shops, schools, and recreation facilities. With this arrangement, automobile and pedestrian traffic were separated, and no home was more than 400 feet from either a park or a major roadway. In contrast to a conventional residential arrangement, the Radburn plan created enough financial savings by limiting roads and utility lines to pay for the cost of the central park.

As part of a systematic attempt to "create an efficient method of community production that would promote both family and friendship," the City Housing Corporation set up the Radburn Association, a nonprofit, non-stock association supported by annual fees paid by all residents.[12] The association's function was to provide services such as sewage disposal, garbage collection, street lighting, and policing; to interpret and enforce the building restrictions; and to hold in trust all of the parkland

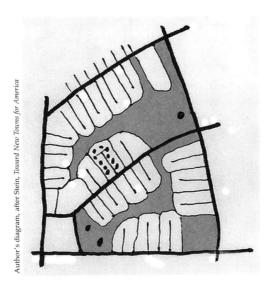

Author's diagram, after Stein, Toward New Towns for America

Figure 2.2. *Clarence Stein believed that Radburn, New Jersey, owed its success to its physical layout—the green center and the shared facilities made it easy and convenient for people to see, meet, and interact with one another.*

and the community facilities, which in the early 1930s included swimming pools, tennis courts, basketball courts, and an archery plaza. The board of trustees of the Radburn Association consisted of appointed civic leaders and members of the City Housing Corporation. Over time, it was expected that residents would join the board and eventually take over. The trustees hired a town manager, chosen on the basis of his executive and managerial qualifications, to handle the day-to-day administration of Radburn.

Planners originally intended that the town should attract a complete range of income groups and be "a microcosm of the larger society." But this failed for two reasons. First, the cost of building and maintaining a home in Radburn proved too expensive for working-class families. Also, realtors employed by the developers thought shared values and experiences were necessary for a smoothly functioning, attractive community. They targeted people with similar backgrounds and interests, meaning they discouraged Jews and blacks from moving to the town. The first town manager explained, "We tried to get people who fit together."[13] In the end, Radburn became a thoroughly middle-class community of young, college-educated residents. The men were mostly salesmen, engineers, teachers, and junior executives—all with a similar income, education level, and religious background. Many commuted to New York City, about 12 miles away.

Within two months of the first family moving in, residents had formed the Radburn Citizens' Association.[14] The association had 17 committees, whose purposes were to provide an open forum for discussing questions of community interest, exchange information about community activities, give residents a voice in dealing with the development company, and foster the organization of various clubs for education, entertainment, and athletics.[15] The Radburn Association provided facilities for these activities and leadership for managing recreational programs, and sent out questionnaires to discover the interests and skills of the residents.

Most residents participated in one or more of these organized activities, which led Robert Hudson, who was the assistant to the manager for community activities, to write in 1934, "[The community is so] thoroughly planned in all its social and other functions that there is scarcely any work left for the church, except in the field of spiritual welfare," and "It is indeed an unusual person or family that does not grow in community mindedness in such an environment."[16]

TWIN OAKS COMMUNITY, LOUISA, VIRGINIA, 1967

The Twin Oaks Community is located on a 450-acre farm about 35 miles southeast of Charlottesville, Virginia.[17] Eight people, mostly college dropouts, founded the community. The founders had corresponded with one another about their hopes for a better world and their wish to live in a cooperative society of happy, productive, and open-minded people. They modeled the community after the fictional society in behaviorist B. F. Skinner's novel *Walden Two*, in which individual members contribute everything they own and families give over the care of their children to the collective.[18] Over the course of its history, Twin Oaks has adopted a more relaxed philosophy, but a great many decisions that affect the individual are still made collectively.

The community derives its income from the manufacture and sale of rope hammocks, tofu, and soy foods, and from a book-indexing service. Twin Oaks produces much of its own vegetables, meat, and milk, and does most of its own machine-repair work. Incoming members give much of what they own to the community—this is negotiated when they join. Each member is required to work a certain number of hours each week for the community. In the early days, each job was assigned a certain number of labor credits depending on how difficult or how disagreeable it was, but now all jobs are counted as equal. Members may decide which jobs they are willing to undertake, but all must do kitchen duty. They receive no payment for their work, but they receive a small amount of pocket money each week; and if they earn additional credits, they may either be paid for them or apply them to their vacation time.

Community facilities are an important focus of life at Twin Oaks. They include the community center, with its communal dining room (where members take most of their meals), mailboxes, and lounge; small meeting rooms and kitchens in the residence buildings; indoor and outdoor recreation facilities scattered throughout the property; and workshops and fields where members work together. Members reside in several buildings. Each adult member has a private bedroom (couples have the option of sharing), but young children share rooms, and all use communal bathrooms. Each residence building houses several living groups, each with its own distinctive character and the right to screen applicants for membership. These residences function much like college dormitories, in which members look after the shared spaces (each residence has its own lounge or meeting room and a kitchen) and arrange occasional group meals and get-togethers.

The community provides for the basic needs of its members, including health care and education. Almost everything in the community belongs to the collective. Members use communally owned cars, vans, and bicycles, and they get clothing from a common pool. There are no television sets—members feel television is a pipeline for values and products that the community is trying to avoid—but movies are viewed on communally owned DVD players. Members participate in a wide range of activities such as dance, meditation, juggling, literature discussions, and the staging of musicals. Members celebrate each change of season and the anniversary of their founding. They also host special events that serve outsiders, including regular tours and the annual Communities Conference.

The overall direction of the community lies in the hands of a board of three planners, who serve 18-month rotating terms. The planners try to reconcile each person's wishes with whatever needs to be accomplished (so that, in effect, all work is voluntary) and make sure that the work is divided equally among the membership. They deal with sensitive questions having to do with the community's ideology; and they appoint and oversee a group of managers, who are each in charge of a particular area of work—there are, for example, managers for visitors, labor, animals, construction, garden, food, clothing,

Figure 2.3. *Residents of Twin Oaks, Virginia, observe Beltane, an ancient May Day festival that celebrates the height of spring and the flowering of life.*

and health. The managers make the majority of important decisions, which are conveyed in the form of suggestions rather than orders, and are guided by the opinions and desires of the members acting as a whole, who can overrule the decisions of the managers and also of the planners. This level of participation requires clear channels of communication, agreed-upon procedures for conducting meetings, and a lively respect for precedent.

Twin Oaks attracts people who are discouraged by and want to escape from the outside world, as well as people who are searching for meaningful relationships and a sense of community. Residents who have difficulty getting along or who cannot attract a mate are unlikely to stay for long. The community accepts new members of different ages, races, sexual orientations, and religious persuasions, but all must subscribe to the idea of a simple way of life.

The community's philosophy is to place priority on communal living, respect for nature, peaceful coexistence, and finding human-scale solutions to the problems of land use, food production, energy conservation, and appropriate use of technology. They place a high value on cooperation and the ability to get along (the use of negative words is discouraged) instead of personal ambition; they believe in treating everyone in an equal, fair, and caring manner, without racial or sexual discrimination; and they do not engage in violence (spanking children is taboo) or drugs. Members must obtain permission from the membership before conceiving or adopting a child, as there is a limit to the number of children that the community can afford to support. In addition, they must agree to raise their children to respect the general values and norms of the community.

People who are interested in joining must live in Twin Oaks for three weeks as visitors. If they decide to apply for membership, they must submit to an exhaustive interview, and then leave the community for a minimum of 10 days while the members decide whether or not to admit them. If the community admits an individual, there is a six-month provisional membership period. If a person is accepted for full membership, he or she must sign an agreement that formalizes the financial arrangements that have been made.

The population of Twin Oaks has fluctuated from a minimum of eight people to a maximum of 100. In 2010, there were 85 adults—predominantly white, and roughly the same number of men and women—and 15 children. Twin Oaks was listed in the 2006 Directory of the Fellowship for Intentional Community, along with 1,142 other North American groups whose members share primary values and a concern about such things as ecology, equality, appropriate technology, spirituality, pursuit of global peace, and self-sufficiency.[19] The central tenets of the intentional community movement include voluntary participation, beginning before the design of the housing and continuing through its management, and the inclusion of community members in all matters of governance.

SEASIDE, FLORIDA, 1982

Seaside is a resort town in Walton County that is built on 80 acres of land on highway C-30A, a narrow, two-lane connector that runs along the Gulf Coast of Florida between Fort Walton Beach and Panama City.[20] Seaside's founder, Robert Davis, wanted to recreate the small towns he remembered as a child. With his architects, Andrés Duany and Elizabeth Plater-Zyberk, he studied the vernacular architecture of the region and concluded that the small-town character he was looking for depended not only on the design of the houses but also on the relationship of the houses to one another and to other elements of the town. Davis consulted Léon Krier, an advocate of traditional town design, who suggested that the area of the site should allow everyone to be within a quarter mile of the center—a distance one can comfortably walk to work or shop.[21]

The resulting master plan created a pedestrian-friendly environment, with a town center (known as Central Square) that provides the necessities of daily life within walking distance of home. The square is bounded on one side by the highway and on the other three sides by stores with apartments above them. The stores are intended to serve local residents, but they could not survive without customers from out of town. Three radial roads extend into the residential area: One is an avenue with a wide planted median, the second is a formal place with stores and upper-level apartments, and the third loops around a school site. A network of streets and footpaths connects the radial roads and comprises the infill. The streets are narrow, paved in brick, lined with trees, and designed to favor pedestrians. The footpaths are surfaced with crushed shells.

In 2000, the town had 45 merchants and more than 300 houses. It had pools, tennis courts, a croquet lawn, a health club, banks, a post office, business services, and meeting facilities. The planners' original intention was to accommodate a wide range of income levels, but property values rose to a point where most of the people who worked in Seaside could not afford to live there. Buyers came from all over the globe; the majority of them were in residence only seasonally. During the rest of the year, vacationers and conference attendees rented the empty houses. In 2010, for example, fewer than 20 families were in residence full-time, and there were some 50,000 accommodation nights.[22] The town functions much like a holiday hotel, with a central office handling all booking and management, including the rental of electric cars and bicycles.

The Seaside design has two main elements: a master plan and a building code. The plan locates the streets, public areas, and building lots. The code defines and places different building types, each with its own requirements for yards, porches, outbuildings, parking, and building heights.

Members of an architectural committee review all plans and color schemes. They may relax the requirements of the code for special sites: Those that are considered to be gateways or focal points may be permitted greater height or greater freedom of placement on the lot, or the owners may be encouraged to include a special feature, such as a bay window, a tower, or a dome. A creative director and a marketing consultant help to coordinate the overall appearance. The effect is to reproduce the look of a small 19-century American town.

Seaside exemplifies many of the principles of the new urbanism movement in its design: a range of housing types with front porches, a prominent civic center, a mix of uses, a modified grid street network, narrow streets, higher density housing with shallow front setbacks, and a return to walkable, active streets.[23] Designers believe that these features will "draw people out of their private realms to stroll and loiter with their

Figure 2.4. *The houses in a typical street in Seaside, Florida, are required to be low, freestanding, and wood framed; the roofs have to be covered with metal and gently pitched, with exposed rafters; and there must be deep overhangs over the mandatory front porches. Houses must be painted in pastel colors, with square or vertical windows and functional shutters. The landscaping must use only sand and native scrub. Each house must have a picket fence, with no single fence pattern repeated on any one street.*

neighbors."[24] According to Peter Katz, the overriding goal of the Seaside designers was to foster a strong sense of community.[25] *Seaside Times*, the local newspaper, gives a great deal of space to articles about the philosophy of the town, stating, "More than ever, we need the roots of community to ground us in this high-speed world. Seaside does this by providing the setting and infrastructure to sustain the community and nurture its growth."[26]

In the attempt to reproduce the appearance of a small town, there is the hope that old-town architectural styles will generate corresponding community values, and "because certain ideas lead to certain looks, style and ideology are inevitably associated. For this reason, traditional architecture may no longer be considered simply in its own terms, but as representative of a traditional outlook and all that implies."[27] One of the mottos of

Seaside is "The new town. The old ways." A study of Seaside, which includes interviews with owners, renters, and workers, concludes that the design of the town helps people form emotional attachments; the architecture provides opportunities for people to engage with neighbors and creates a feeling of membership among residents; and the town philosophy encourages the development of a sense of community.[28]

Seaside residents and representatives of the developer form a council, which is the town's unofficial local government. The council, supported by an assessment levied against each resident, helps to enforce the building code and oversees the maintenance of the streets and public places. Founder Robert Davis, who has lived at least part-time in Seaside, presides over nearly every aspect of the town's development from the design of stationery to recommending the selection of entrées at the local restaurant. He has been known to stop a building in progress if it did not complete his desired visual composition. Davis set up the Seaside Institute, a nonprofit organization, to encourage artists and organize concerts, exhibits, festivals, and literary events for residents and visitors. The institute, which also sponsors residency programs for scholars, runs forums and conferences to promote the new urbanism movement.

SUMMARY

Research has shown that residents are more likely to form a community if they share the same values and beliefs—that is, if they are homogeneous (see chapter 1 for a review of this research). In practice, a homogeneous neighborhood is generally one in which most people come from the same socioeconomic group.

The development histories in this chapter show how communities can be designed to achieve homogeneity, and how different projects use different methods to attract or exclude targeted groups, including advertising by developers and screening by realtors or the residents themselves.

The developments in this chapter also show other elements that have community-generating potential: community organizations, institutions that develop greater interdependence between an individual resident and the group (Twin Oaks is an extreme example), a physical environment that presents a distinctive appearance and identity, institutions such as schools and churches, and parks and squares that encourage leisure-time activities. I will address these elements more fully in subsequent chapters. Each of them works more smoothly with a homogeneous group of residents.

CHAPTER 3

Community Organizations

In this little restaurant . . . the regulars greeted one another with not more than a discreet nod—for, although they had seen each other every single day at lunchtime for years, they had not been introduced.

—Georges Simenon[1]

A community organization creates opportunities and reasons for residents to meet one another and work together. The discussions in this chapter focus on local organizations as a fundamental element of community. They show that communities have different agendas: In Carmel-by-the-Sea, California, the organizations are concerned with art and the preservation of the natural environment; in Levittown, New York, with the provision of services and programs; in Celebration, Florida, quite explicitly with the creation of community; and in Rosebank, Baltimore, with little more than property maintenance.

CARMEL-BY-THE-SEA, CALIFORNIA, 1902

The city of Carmel-by-the-Sea, on the Monterey Peninsula in California, is located on the site of an early Spanish mission whose stone church, established in 1793, still stands.[2] The town itself dates from 1900, when James Franklin Devendorf, a real estate developer, bought the land, then a pine forest, and formed the Carmel Development Company. He acted as the town's informal mayor until its incorporation in 1916. Devendorf wanted to create a community that respected and enhanced the natural setting. In a brochure advertising Carmel-by-the-Sea, he wrote:

> The settlement has been built on the theory that people of aesthetic (as broadly defined) taste would settle in a town of Carmel's naturally aesthetic beauties provided all public enterprises were addressed toward preventing man and his civilized ways from unnecessarily marring the natural beauty so lavishly displayed here.[3]

Devendorf had inherited a grid plan from the previous owner, but he reoriented the grid in order to save natural features of the landscape. He set buildings into the forest with minimal destruction of the existing trees, and he paid close attention to the natural topography and the site's relationship to Carmel Bay. He planted pines along the roads and Monterey cypresses along the sea cliffs, and he gave trees to new buyers to plant on their land.[4]

Devendorf marketed the area to people he characterized as having good taste. He sent a mimeographed letter to "the School Teachers of California and other Brain Workers at Indoor Employment" offering them land at bargain prices, with low down payments and low monthly installments. In 1905, the president of Stanford University, David Starr Jordan, and a number of faculty members bought lots and built houses on a street known as "Professors' Row." Writers, playwrights, and poets were attracted to Carmel-by-the-Sea and documented its natural beauty. Carmel-by-the-Sea gained a reputation as a place of eccentric, artistic people. In 1910, the *Los Angeles Times* published this tongue-in-cheek description:

> Of late it has become the magnetizing center for writers, near writers, notsonear [sic] writers, distant writers, poets, poetines, artists, daubers, sloydists, and those aspiring ladies who end up their days smearing up with paint what would otherwise

be very serviceable pieces of canvas. In addition there are at least 20 college professors, a club of well-meaning neophytes of the arts-and-crafts, esoteric Yogi, New Thoughters, Emmanuel Movers—and last (but not least, O Lord) the dramatists.[5]

That same year, the residents formed the outdoor Forest Theater on a bowl-shaped hillside, among the pines. Devendorf provided the land rent free and later sold it to the theater at a bargain price. Local writers wrote original plays, and members of the community participated in the productions. Two other drama societies were established. Residents formed the Arts and Crafts Club, whose regular exhibitions became a high point in the artistic life of the town. Their clubhouse was used as a community center for lectures, classes, and theatricals, and for a summer school of the arts, which continued into the mid-1920s.

In 1927, residents formed the Carmel Art Association to help local artists exhibit and sell their work. The organization also arranged social events for the community. That same year, residents formed the Carmel Music Society to sponsor chamber music concerts and recitals. The concerts eventually became the annual three-day Carmel Bach Festival, which now attracts visitors from all over the United States.

In 1916, the 550 permanent residents of Carmel-by-the-Sea decided to incorporate, and Carmel-by-the-Sea officially became a city. One of the first pieces of legislation was an ordinance prohibiting the cutting of city-owned trees. When, in 1922, a developer proposed building a large resort hotel on the beach dunes, residents protested and persuaded Devendorf to sell the land to them instead. A writer to the *Carmel Pine Cone*, a weekly publication founded in 1915 and still in publication, commented: "It says that Carmel's first thought is not for the humbug of 'progress' but for the beauty, dignity, and reticence that mean character. It says . . . that the placid homey life rather than 'good business' are the town ideals."[6]

Carmel-by-the-Sea is known for its quaint houses, tended gardens, trees, flower beds along the public roads, stores, art galleries, and restaurants around fountain courtyards. The houses have no street numbers and no mail addresses. Instead, they have names, such as Tinkerbell; or people give an address such as "the second house southwest of Seventh and Camino Real." Residents do not have door-to-door mail delivery, choosing instead to pick up their mail at the post office, which serves as a social meeting place. In 1926, there was an ordinance to number the houses, but it was ignored and finally repealed in 1940. In 2000, the U.S. Postal Service announced that it would assign street numbers and offer free home delivery. This provoked an angry outcry from Carmel-by-the-Sea residents. One resident is reported to have said, "The post office creates connection between people—it's 'I had a dream about you last night. Are you all right?' Well, the mailman is not going to do that."[7]

As the town grew in popularity, property values increased dramatically, and there was an increase in the number of expensive second/vacation homes. In 2002, more than half of all the housing units were absentee owned, and many long-time residents had difficulty finding affordable housing. The

Wayne Holding, courtesy of Bay Publishing Co.

Figure 3.1. *Patricia Brown describes Carmel-by-the-Sea, California, as "a town that cultivates eccentricity like a rare organic tomato" and its architecture as "Later Troll style" (Brown, "Fighting for a Carrier-free Zone"). The buildings reflect the artistic character of the community.*

preponderance of seasonal and recreational residents was seen to diminish the essential character of the town and the stability of the community.[8]

Preserving the unique qualities of Carmel-by-the-Sea has been a continuing concern of the community. In 1946, Carmel-by-the-Sea created a planning commission, which wrote into law a number of traditions that had been previously observed informally but had become increasingly threatened by the economic pressures of tourism. They regulated advertising signs, banned outdoor electric signs, required motels to provide off-street parking and planting, imposed building height limitations and setback requirements, and forbade sidewalks and street paving in residential areas. As a nod to its uneven street and sidewalk surfaces, the town passed a "high heels" ordinance in the 1920s that requires a permit to wear shoes with heels higher than two inches and with less than one square inch of bearing surface. In 2001, responding to the displacement of distinctive local stores by larger shopping centers, and to speculators paying large sums of money for the town's old cottages only to tear them down and replace them with full-size "monster" houses, the planning commission drafted a set of design standards aimed at retaining the simple residential character of the city as "a village in the forest."

LEVITTOWN, LONG ISLAND, NEW YORK, 1947

In 1947, Levitt and Sons, a company of housing developers, bought 300 acres of land near Island Trees, on Long Island, New York.[9] The land had previously been used for potato farming. The Levitts had no long-term housing development plan. They did not know from one year to the next how the housing market was going to be. They began with a plan to build 2,000 four-room houses. By the end of 1948, they had built 6,000 houses, and by 1951, they had built 17,500.

About halfway through the development process, the Levitts realized that they were building more than a subdivision—they were creating a community—and so they built seven village greens, or commercial areas. Each was designed to serve between 2,000 and 4,000 families and was meant to be used as a center of community life. Near the greens, the Levitts placed parks, playgrounds, open spaces, and often a swimming pool—facilities that could be expected to attract customers to the shops. They built a community meeting hall; they made several parcels of land available at cost for the construction of schools (the local municipality was responsible for building them and developing the curriculum); and they donated three lots to religious bodies on condition that they build within a year. The facilities had no clear geographic relationship to neighborhoods or to one another.[10]

The houses were set on curving streets, with staggered setbacks. The first houses were all rental units. They were painted in several colors, and there were slight variations in appearance; models included the Lookout Cape, the Snug Harbor Cape, the Green Hills, and the Mariner. Each house had a lawn in the front and an identical number of shade trees, fruit trees, and shrubs; there were rules about what could be redecorated and what could not; and there were restrictions on fences (which were seen as "complete barriers to friendship"), garages, accessory buildings, and the use of outdoor wash lines.

The later houses were offered for ownership; they came with covenants that required the owners to obtain approval for all colors and materials used in renovations. The Levitts used local newspapers to give residents information, instructions (for example, about emergency parking of cars during a snowstorm), suggestions (such as tips for proper care of floors and attics), and admonishments (one notice warned against hanging wash on weekends, when prospective buyers would be visiting).

There was no intentional attempt to design neighborhoods in Levittown, but residents sometimes used the word *neighborhood* loosely, to refer to a unit of subdivision, an area defined by minor political boundaries, and sometimes to an area whose street names have a common theme—there are, for example, the celestial section (Comet, Solar, Meridian, Satellite, and Polaris Lanes), the horsey set (Saddle, Bridle, and Harness Lanes), and the tradesmen's streets (Barrister, Cleaner, Stonecutter, and Rigger Lanes).[11]

The Levitts marketed their houses to middle-class workers, rather than the upper class. Prospective residents had to be white, earn more than a certain income, and have been war veterans.[12] The early residents of Levittown found that this degree of background similarity made it easy for them to form friendships. The houses were built in subdivisions of about 300 units, and all of the houses in each subdivision were completed and occupied at about the same time. This meant that all the residents in a subdivision moved in at approximately the same time, so together they were newcomers, cut off from their previous social networks, looking to make new friends, and seeking to develop new institutions. As one resident recalled:

> We were all pioneers, we were in the same situation, we all came in together. It's like the Senate. No matter what party, you don't attack another senator; it's a club. We had the same kinds of desires and needs, fought the same kinds of battles; no matter what sides we were on, there was a camaraderie.[13]

Courtesy of Levittown History Collection

Figure 3.2. *The Fourth of July parade in Levittown, New York, reminds residents that the community was founded by ex-servicemen and their families.*

Critics of Levittown complained that the unrelieved uniformity of the houses would discourage the formation of community, but in the view of some residents, the physical environment had little to do with it. As one claimed, "You know, Levitt built the houses . . . It's the vets that moved in, that created Levittown . . . It's their values and their energy that created this community."[14] Many residents expanded and redesigned their houses, and they did much of the work through a combination of do-it-yourself labor and barter. People spoke about the pleasures of working with their neighbors as they enclosed carports, added dormers and ells, and traded tools and supplies. Today, there are so few unmodified Levitt houses remaining that the Smithsonian Institution is reported to be looking to acquire one for its collection.[15]

Early on, Levittown residents became active in local politics and in creating the curriculum and administration of the local school. They built a library and formed a volunteer fire department. They formed a community association (which had little governing authority), a tenants' council, an American Legion group, a veterans' committee, and other social organizations, using homes, churches, and taverns as meeting places. In a short time, a hundred or so organizations had sprung up.

Herbert Gans's study of a later Levitt Brothers development (Levittown in New Jersey) is an insightful record of the way that people who are all strangers to a place and to one another go about creating new organizations and institutions.[16] Gans found that when people first moved into the new town, they began looking among their neighbors for playmates for their children, and then they looked for companions for themselves. They met while walking up and down the street with baby carriages or while working on their lawns, and they would exchange bits of personal and family information, looking for common backgrounds or interests. Every contact could advance people closer to friendship, or it could bring out differences that would indicate that friendship was not possible. They started trading invitations to share coffee and began to organize parties, such as card, Tupperware, Fourth of July, Halloween, and Christmas gatherings. The block social system stabilized very quickly; relationships ranged from close friendship to open hostility, but most people chose friendly coexistence. Standards of lawn care and norms of social entertaining were agreed upon. Neighbors pitched in to help in cases of accident or illness.

The first people to find social lives outside the block were minorities and people who had a difficult time finding immediate neighbors with similar cultural and social interests. They began to look for friends among people they met at communitywide meetings or fund drives; they joined voluntary associations such as drama societies, art clubs, folk dance clubs, great books clubs, or babysitting groups. Jewish families met to discuss the formation of a synagogue. Women formed separate clubs catering to the needs of older women, women interested in civic activities, women with traveling husbands, foreign wives, and British wives. Some residents founded groups to address local needs—an emergency ambulance squad, a ham radio club, the Citizens' Association for Public Schools, and the Youth Sports Association. Some groups, such as those of new residents who felt that the older groups were exclusive, arose in opposition to already established ones.

The various groups and organizations functioned as sorting mechanisms that divided and segregated people by their interests and socioeconomic, educational, and religious differences. Community leaders emerged, some motivated by a strong personal need to be leaders, others because their livelihood required them to meet people and to become known. Leaders of one group were asked to help with others, and so interlocking directorates were created, with the same people and their friends holding leadership positions in several groups.

Gans makes several insightful points. People who find themselves surrounded by strangers in new environments are unusually open to meeting new people and forming new friendships. This is particularly true of mothers with young children. The first residents in a new development think of themselves as pioneers together. They establish social connections very quickly, but these are not necessarily lasting bonds, and as residents settle in and broaden their interests, their ties to the local community may become weaker. In the early years, the pioneering feeling can be strong enough to overshadow the effects of a physical setting that is not designed to foster a sense of community.

The Levittown developments illustrate how people identify and distinguish among neighborhoods even when there are no physical boundaries between them. To contrast this example, in the Baltimore neighborhood study referred to earlier, residents of one neighborhood said that they knew when they were leaving their area and entering another by changes in the condition of the houses, the make of parked cars, and the appearance of people in the streets.[17] The story of the Levittowns also suggests that community organizations will almost inevitably happen if one brings similar people to live together in the same area. Residents will form them without assistance from community designers.

CELEBRATION, FLORIDA, 1996

The Celebration Company, a branch of the Walt Disney Company, developed Celebration, Florida.[18] Located five miles south of Walt Disney World, it covers 4,900 acres of land (with approximately the same amount of acreage preserved in wetlands). Celebration is designed to house about 20,000 people, and it was expected to become a paragon for the development of residential communities.[19] The architects of the master plan—Cooper, Robertson & Partners in partnership with Robert A. M. Stern Architects—created what resembles a traditional small American town of the late 19th or early 20th century.

The plan is a fan-shaped grid, with the commercial center of the town at its hinge. The primary access route, Celebration Avenue, leads to a small square with signature buildings such as the town hall, a visitors' center, and the post office. On one side of the square, a one-block shopping street leads through the town's center to the lakefront. The center is the size of three large blocks and offers a small grocery, a bank, apartments, offices, a cinema, several restaurants, gift shops, clothing boutiques, a hotel, and a school. Residents tend to do most of their shopping outside Celebration, and the stores rely heavily on tourists who visit the town as a side trip on their way to or from Disney World. A wide avenue leads away from the center, through the residential area, and terminates at a golf course clubhouse.

The houses in Celebration are a mix of pastel-colored apartments, row houses, and single-family detached houses set close to one another and to the street. Homes have porches and small fenced yards. Andrew Ross, in *The Celebration Chronicles*, writes that this physical arrangement contributes to community by making it virtually impossible not to know one's neighbors. Residents mention the ease with which they interact with neighbors and hail passersby on the street. Without extensive backyards, children mingle and play in the larger areas provided by parks and public spaces.[20] Frantz and Collins remark that when it comes to community involvement, Celebration's layout is barrier free.[21]

The houses are required to conform to six approved design styles: Classical, Victorian, Colonial Revival, Coastal, Mediterranean, and French. For each style, a pattern book prescribes the preferred placement and design in relation to the street and the size of the lot and house. It shows the correct proportions for everything from massing and setback to the details of fences, depth of porches, and recommended exterior material and color. It addresses the spacing between dormers, doors, porches, columns, and bays.[22]

Prospective residents are required to sign the 100-page Declaration of Covenants, Conditions, and Restrictions, which regulates the outside physical appearance of the community. This document prescribes the types and locations of trees and shrubs to be planted in the yards. It requires residents to keep their houses painted, maintain their yards, and have white or off-white linings on all window curtains visible from the street. If a house is repainted, the color of the exterior paint, if it differs from the original color, has to be reviewed and approved, and no colors other than white may be repeated in adjacent houses. Residents are not permitted to hang washing outdoors. They are not permitted to park a recreational vehicle in front of their building or park more than two vehicles per housing unit in the street or alley. Each house can hold only one garage sale a year and can post only one political sign, measuring no more than 18 by 24 inches, in the yard (and only for 45 days before an election). For Sale signs are not permitted to be posted on the property.[23]

The Celebration Company set up the Celebration Foundation, a nonprofit institution, in order to facilitate community initiatives.

It also set up the Celebration Residential Owners Association (to be controlled by the company until the town is three-quarters completed) to enforce the covenants and restrictions. The Celebration Company appointed a community services manager, who acts as the town's unofficial mayor. The manager organizes and provides seed money for community groups, clubs, and branches of national organizations, including a garden club, the Celebrators Club for retirees and semiretirees, a Rotary Club, a chamber of commerce council, a children's playgroup, scouting, Indian Guides, and the Celebration Players. The Celebration Foundation hosts the parks and recreation office, which sponsors recreation programs. The foundation also runs a volunteer center for recruiting and placing resident volunteers in the town's clubs and community groups. It runs orientation programs for new residents, organizes community picnics and yard sales, and does outreach work in the local county.[24] A computer network links all of the houses to the various offices and organizations in the town. Known as My Front Porch, it provides information

Courtesy of Celebration Foundation

Figure 3.3. *The Fourth of July parade in Celebration, Florida, forms an association between the new community and long-standing traditions. The photo is from 2002.*

about community activities, reminding residents that they are expected to volunteer and participate in local events, activities, and festivals.[25]

Celebration was widely advertised as an alternative to the Lonelyville of suburbia.[26] The first residents came from all over the country, attracted by the promise of an old-time community, the reputation of the Walt Disney Company as exceptional managers, and the promise of an excellent and innovative school system. Most believed that it offered the potential for a better life. "It's almost as if our neighbors had been chosen."[27]

However, residents had no shared memories or traditions to bind them together as a community. The Celebration Company tried to create a collective memory by developing an elaborate orientation program known as Celebration Traditions, which suggested a direct line of descent from the prehistoric occupants of Central Florida to the residents of Celebration. The program was later dropped when incoming residents

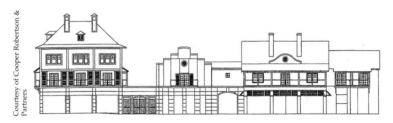

Courtesy of Cooper Robertson & Partners

Figure 3.4. *The Celebration Company describes this building as follows: "The connected structures at 715 Bloom Street is [sic] designed to look as if it had started as three separate commercial structures with 'flats' above, which had become connected over time, in the natural evolution of the town, to produce a single building with three very different facades . . . The corner building, a vertical building, taller than the others and painted gray and white with dark blue shutters, is what the architect calls 'high style, almost New England.' Next to it, connected through a small courtyard, is a yellow building with a classical American false front and a stepped gable, that 'would have been an insurance company.' The third building is a darker color, terra cotta with black trim, and is intended, the architects say, to seem 'slightly aged,' as if it were the oldest of the three and thus 'more inviting, more accessible'" (The Celebration Company, Downtown Celebration, 7).*

complained of indoctrination.[28] The Celebration Company attempted to trigger northerners' shared seasonal memories by setting up machines to blow fake leaves and snow (made of bubble bath and window cleaner) on Market Street at the beginning of fall and winter.[29] They also designed new buildings that reflected a fictitious past.[30]

While Levittown showed that if similar people move into an area, they will create community organizations by themselves, Celebration shows that developer-initiated organizations can accelerate and shape the community-building process. Community organizations are both generators and expressions of community.

THE COMMUNITY OF ROSEBANK, BALTIMORE, 1970s–1980s

The Community of Rosebank (not its real name) is a condominium development of 104 town houses, begun in the 1970s and completed in the late 1980s.[31] It sits on just more than 13 acres of land, fenced off from the surrounding neighborhoods. A sign that reads "The Community of Rosebank" marks the entrance. The road passes between two gateposts (although it is not a gated community), winds around a central swimming pool and clubhouse, and leads to five clusters of houses. Each cluster consists of several strings of row houses, adjacent to or grouped around a parking court. One resident distinguishes the groups by giving them names: Eddie-side (Eddie is a resident), Curve-side, Downhill, Students, Neighbors, Older, Stony Spring, and Entrance.

The houses were designed to be moderately priced and comfortable. They have different floor plans, and the elevation of each varies, but they are clearly all of a piece. The houses are finished in beige-colored stucco, and each has an open yard at the front and a small fenced yard at the back. They are considered good investments for first-time home buyers. The residents are mainly educated, high-income professionals, including doctors, scientists, educators, lawyers, and entrepreneurs. A relatively high proportion of the residents are foreign-born, and there are a number of young children. Seven

Mary Worth cartoon strip, July 14, 2000, courtesy of and © North America Syndicate

Figure 3.5. *It may take more than a cluster of houses, a condominium association, and a pool to create a community. A resident of Rosebank, Baltimore, describes his development as "a community geographically, not necessarily in other matters."*

to 10 of the houses are rented, some to college students. Most residents work, but there are several who are not employed, most of them retirees.

All property owners are required to pay a monthly condominium fee to the Rosebank Homeowners Association, which owns and maintains the common facilities: the road, pool, clubhouse, water lines, and common spaces. The association has a 10-member board, with officers elected for a three-year period. There is, however, little interest in serving on the board, and although meetings are open to all residents, only two or three non–board members show up on a regular basis. The president of the association observed, "Most people in this community are clueless that there's a board of directors unless they happen to read their newsletter . . . Unless there is an issue, I'm sure most people here don't really care."

Most of the money from the condominium fees is used to pay a private firm to manage the property. This firm is responsible for planting the flowerbeds, cutting the grass, removing snow, repairing streetlights, maintaining the infrastructure, resurfacing streets, doing general repairs, and operating the pool. The home owners association established covenants and restrictions that are intended to protect property values and that govern all modifications to the exterior of the units, including choice of paint color. The association also deals with such matters as parking, trash, and neighbor-to-neighbor and owner-to-tenant disputes. It leases the clubhouse for private parties. It organizes programs at the pool and occasional garage sales and community cleanups.

Residents as a whole are not particularly interested in community events. They are friendly, and in the summer, they socialize at the pool, or meet and talk on the sidewalks in front of their houses as they walk their dogs or work in their yards. However, a number of residents think of themselves as members of the adjacent, more established community, and people with children are more connected with one another than with their other coresidents.

Residents speak about Rosebank as a place for "easy living," "a private oasis within the city," and "a bedroom community with conveniences." It is low maintenance, ideal for busy working people who are absorbed in their jobs and families.

Rosebank differs from the other communities in this chapter in that the home owners association does little to bring residents together. However, residents do not seem to want to come together. There is a general belief that a strong sense of community and strong community organizations are better than weak ones. This may not always be the case. Rosebank residents look to their residential area more for privacy than for togetherness.

SUMMARY

The four development histories of Carmel-by-the-Sea, Levittown, Celebration, and Rosebank illustrate different kinds of community organizations, ways in which they can form, and how an effective organization can generate a sense of community. In Carmel-by-the-Sea, residents created an organization with the encouragement and support of the developer. In Levittown, residents themselves created a community organization. In Celebration, the organization was created and staffed by the developer, who worked to drum up resident participation. In Rosebank, the developer set up a single-purpose organization and required home owners to be members. Some of these organizations were supported by a newsletter, newspaper, or, in the case of Celebration, a computer network. Some required special facilities, such as a clubhouse, theater, swimming pool, school, or, in the case of Carmel-by-the-Sea, city offices and a post office.

One may question why, if the residents of Levittown can form organizations with little or no outside help, we should include organization building as part of a community design. My answer is that unless residents are like-minded and see themselves as pioneers, simply bringing them together may not create a community (see the study of mixed income housing in chapter 8). The following quotations illustrate the points that bringing residents together does not necessarily lead to interaction and that interaction does not necessarily lead to creating a sense of community.

> Last summer I was much struck by a friend's attitude towards her new neighbour in a north Oxford suburb. "Irritating man," she exclaimed, "he doesn't know how to behave in a garden." What she meant was that he would insist on talking over the garden wall instead of steadfastly ignoring her presence just a few metres away. We find that mentality in London is much the same. There is an urban art of avoiding catching the eye, a kind of downward glance as one proceeds with hanging out the washing or pruning the roses.[32]

I have lived for the last 30 years in a building housing people in the arts [and] have developed a nodding acquaintance with some tenants and am friendlier with others in varying degrees. The other day, I got into an elevator with two other original tenants, an actor I've seen on screen but whose name I don't know, and a woman I know by name.

"Hi, Sheila," I greeted her. She nodded and smiled.

"Is your name Sheila?" the actor asked.

She nodded.

"But," he said, "I've been calling you Lillian for years and you never corrected me."

"Yes," she replied, "and you never heard me answer you, either, did you?"[33]

Rosebank exemplifies the fact that some communities have only the most superficial of social ties. It teaches us that not all residents are interested in building community. They may fail to interact because they prefer privacy; fear crime (people are less inclined to interact if they feel that they will be put in danger); are busy (people are less likely to interact if they are hurrying to get something done); or are away from home much of the time (families in which both parents work may find little time to socialize with their neighbors). Some people do not want to be friends with their neighbors and are content with an organization whose concerns are limited to maintaining property and protecting value.

The communities in this chapter, to a greater or lesser extent, were also designed to attract people with similar values, provide a range of facilities and services, and develop and celebrate local traditions. They have other features noted in chapter 1—notably, they cater to long-term residents and they have a distinctive physical appearance. Two additional design features are worthy of consideration: facilities that cater particularly to leisure-time uses, and clear physical boundaries. Both of these are found in Rosebank.

CHAPTER 4

Suitable Physical Settings

First, let our markets be well built, and our cottage areas well laid out; then there will soon grow up such a full civic life, such a joy and pride in the city as will seek expression in adornment.

—Raymond Unwin[1]

The informal relationship of houses, the ease with which one can cross a couple of lawns and call out "Who's home?" has affected the social and civic expression of the people.

—Clarence Stein[2]

The development histories in this chapter focus on places that encourage local residents to meet and, hopefully, interact. In Riverside, Illinois, public parkland is designed as a gathering place. In Letchworth, in the United Kingdom, the garden city design provides a civic and retail center; the neighborhood unit formula proposes a neighborhood center; Columbia, Maryland, creates a hierarchy of centers at neighborhood, village, and city levels; and Lake Claire Cohousing, Atlanta, includes private courtyards and a common house. Each community design addresses the question of facility management and programming in its own way: In Letchworth, these functions are left entirely to future residents; in Riverside, the designer creates well-designed facilities in the belief that they will entice

57

residents to manage and program them; in Columbia, these functions are assigned to a citywide organization; and in Lake Claire Cohousing they are assigned to committees of residents.

RIVERSIDE, ILLINOIS, 1868

In 1868, Frederick Law Olmsted, designer for the firm of Olmsted, Vaux and Co., completed a plan for a new residential development that he hoped would foster "the harmonious association and co-operation of men in a community."[3] It was called Riverside, and it was situated on 1,600 acres of undeveloped land approximately nine miles south of Chicago, along a commuter train line. The Des Plaines River cuts through the site from north to south, and then turns sharply to the east, where it is joined by a western branch of the same river and continues along the southern boundary of the site. The railroad cuts across the site in an east–west direction.

At the point where the railroad crosses the river, near the passenger station, Olmsted placed a highly visible water tower. A road extended from the station through a chain of small parks to join a parkway to Chicago. The river and the railroad divide the site into several residential sections, each with its own internal parks and playgrounds.

Residents were expected to work and shop in Chicago, and so Olmsted did not design a town center. (Later, the developers added a block of stores and offices, a billiard pavilion, and a hotel.) In total, 700 acres of prime land, including all of the land along both banks of the river, were set aside for drives, walks, and public recreation areas. Olmsted also developed an extensive planting program: By 1871, 47,000 shrubs, 7,000 evergreens, and 32,000 deciduous trees had been planted.

The plan for Riverside included more than 300 residential lots, which were described as being "of liberal dimensions, affording sufficient ground for extended lawns, the cultivation of trees, shrubs, flowers, [and] small fruits . . . beside ample space for a barn remote from the house, and for roads and walks."[4] Olmsted believed that the gardenlike setting would inspire feelings of "leisure, contemplativeness and happy tranquility" and would induce men to become more domesticated by spending more time with their families. He advocated the European custom of promenading—walking for the pure joy of walking, and also to see and be seen—and for that purpose he designed gracefully curving village roads with paved, well-drained surfaces that were usable in all seasons. Street trees kept the paths cool and shaded, and screened the houses from view. In addition, houses were required to have 30-foot setbacks from the road and low hedges and fences along the side property line because, Olmsted wrote,

> We cannot judiciously attempt to control the form of the houses which men shall build, we can only, at most, take care that if they build very ugly and inappropriate houses, they shall not be allowed to force them disagreeably upon our attention when we desire to pass along the road upon which they stand.

These building restrictions were promoted by the development company as "a sure guarantee to every purchaser that no improvements can be made that will in the least detract from the beauty of his own, and will at the same time add materially to the general beauty of the entire neighborhood."[5]

Olmsted did not call the public recreation areas "parks," which he thought of as places where one could be alone with nature, but "public grounds," which, he suggested, would have the character of informal village greens, with scattered croquet and ball courts, playgrounds, seats, and drinking fountains. Along the river, which was eventually dammed for boating and skating, Olmsted planned terraces, balconies, pavilions, a public drive, and walks leading to boat landings. The designer believed that public areas of "refined sylvan beauty and graceful umbraceousness" greatly exceeding what any home owner could provide on his or her own property would lure residents out of their houses to walk, exercise, and learn about nature.

Public grounds would bring families together for open-air gatherings, organized sports games, and fetes, and would provide opportunities for people of different classes to come together as equals. Olmsted believed that in the process of coming together for "easy, friendly, unceremonious greetings, for the enjoyment of change of scene, of cheerful and exhilarating sights and sounds, and of various good cheer," residents

Figure 4.1. *Olmsted's park still brings residents of Riverside, Illinois, together. This picture shows them celebrating the Fourth of July.*

would come to enjoy one another's company. The public grounds would develop civic pride, virtue, and prosperity.

Today, Riverside is an incorporated town with a village president, and it supports a full range of schools, churches, commercial establishments, and community facilities. The town's website lists 27 local fraternal, sport, hobby, cultural, and civic organizations, including a chamber of commerce, the Frederick Law Olmsted Society, and the Riverside Historical Commission.[6]

LETCHWORTH GARDEN CITY, UNITED KINGDOM, 1903

In 1898, Ebenezer Howard published his book, *Tomorrow, a Peaceful Path To Social Reform*. Reprinted in 1902 as *Garden Cities of Tomorrow*, it became the bible of the international garden cities movement.[7] What Howard proposed, in effect, was to stop the creeping expansion of a large city (London, in this case) by creating a ring of interconnected but separate satellite towns, each relatively self-contained and with no more than 30,000 people, separated from the center city and from one another by open country.

Howard's diagram of a satellite town shows a central park and garden, faced by, in his words, "magnificent" civic buildings, including a town hall, concert and lecture hall, theater, library, museum, art gallery, and hospital. This center is surrounded by a glass-enclosed shopping mall. Six residential areas, or wards, radiate out from the town center, each with its own park and playing fields, school, and church. It would be possible for a resident to walk in one direction to the town center, or in the other direction to the railroad station and an adjacent industrial area, and then on to the open country, which would be the source of a constant supply of fresh food.

All of the land would remain common property and would be administered by an elected board of management. The board would collect ground rent from every townsperson and, after the initial land acquisition and construction loans had been repaid, use the surplus rent money, together with any additional money resulting from increases in land value, to make improvements that would benefit all the residents of the town.

In 1903, the Garden City Pioneer Company formed in London to find a site on which to build a garden city following Howard's ideas. The company chose 3,800 acres of land in Hertfordshire, on a rail line that connects with London, about 34 miles away. The town would be called Letchworth, after a small village that existed on the outskirts of the site, and the First Garden City Limited was formed to raise money for its establishment. The company modified Howard's original proposal for resident ownership: It would retain ownership of the land, residents would pay ground rent, investors would receive a limited dividend on their investment, and any profits would go to the company, which would use them to benefit the town as a whole or its individual residents as it saw fit.

First Garden City Ltd. selected the architectural firm of Raymond Unwin and Barry Parker to prepare a plan. The original drawings show a central square, surrounded by civic and religious buildings, connected with a wide processional way to the railroad station and adjoining industrial areas. Axial streets radiate out from the square, so that looking inward, one would see a framed view of a civic building on the square, and looking outward, across the surrounding green belt, a distant village, church steeple, or watchtower. Streets extended from the central square to outlying hamlets, each with a subcenter surrounded by housing.

Building started at a distance from the center, and it was many years before the central square was completed. A temporary railroad station and a golf club opened in 1905. A memorial hall (named after Mrs. Howard) opened in 1906, funded through money-raising events such as bazaars, jumble sales, and dramatic performances. It was used for meetings, social events, a dancing club, lectures, dramatic readings, and later, a girls club (a "place where the girls of Letchworth may meet for healthy

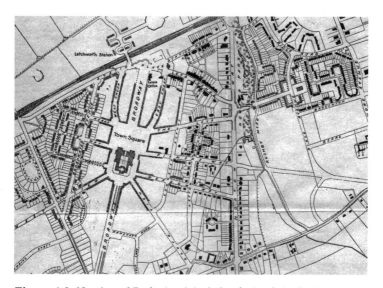

Figure 4.2. *Unwin and Parker's original plan for Letchworth, U.K. The developers did not follow this plan faithfully, but they kept the essential elements. Unwin believed that the town center would be a catalyst for community. Several years later, in 1912, he spoke about "the amorphous mass of humanity . . . beginning to take on a definite relation to the center . . . as particles in a chemical solution group themselves into beautiful crystalline form about some central point of attraction" (Unwin, Warburton Lectures, 1912, quoted in Miller,* Raymond Unwin, *110).*

recreation and have opportunities for companionship and education") that offered courses in dressmaking, cooking, first aid, singing, gymnastics, leatherwork, decorative arts, swimming, and tennis.

In 1905, an engineering company and a printing company moved to Letchworth, followed by other printing and bookbinding works. By 1907, Letchworth boasted approximately 30 shops, four hotels, the Skittles Inn—a pub that did not serve beer—and the Cloisters, a theosophical center and open-air school (where men and women slept in hammocks and took communal meals, and the housework was done by young men in robes and sandals). The Spirella Corset Factory, constructed in 1912, included a café, a fitness center, and a ballroom.

In the early years, the housing lots sold slowly. The first residents were professionals and businessmen with their families. The town attracted people with independent minds who were looking for something new and hoped to invent fresh approaches to religion, art, education, and even agriculture. Advertisements described Letchworth as "a great social experiment of national value." The town became known as a place for zealots, freethinkers, and cranks. Jonathan Glancey writes, "Cockney workers on their Sundays off, booked excursions by train from King's Cross to come and gawk at Letchworth's implausible gathering of quacks, weavers, potters, feminists, yoga fetishists and birth-control fanatics."[8]

The directors of the company, concerned about the effect that this reputation might have on their ability to attract new residents, began to discourage anything that appeared to be out of the ordinary. The new industries brought tradesmen, mechanics, and clerical workers, who arrived with few or none of the eager expectations that the first residents had. Social clubs were formed, followed by the customary church groups, sports clubs, trade unions, and so on. In 1909, a resident commented on the "air of freedom and sociability delightful to notice and still better to experience; societies and institutions sufficient to cater for the tastes of all and sundry; the prevalence of a true spirit of citizenship and social intercourse rarely seen."[9]

All of the houses in Letchworth had gardens, and trees lined the streets. Communal living groups developed. In one such group, small houses were arranged around a green, with

Figure 4.3. *The Letchworth community—including Ebenezer Howard, in the center, wearing a bowler hat—came together to celebrate the coronation of King George V, in 1911.*

a common dining room and kitchen (the use of which was included in the rent). Each resident in turn was responsible for catering midday meals for a period of two weeks. In another group, houses and flats were arranged around a quadrangle, with a common dining area and services. Ebenezer Howard himself lived for several years in one of these precursors of contemporary cohousing.[10]

The company was concerned about the overall appearance of the town and supported its architects' conviction that a town should have a unified and attractive appearance, with "the crystallization of the elements of the village in accordance with a definitely organized life of mutual relations, respect, or service, which gives the appearance of being an organic whole, the home of a community, to what would otherwise be a mere conglomeration of buildings."[11] In order to achieve this "appearance of being an organic whole," prospective builders were given these design suggestions:

The directors of First Garden City Ltd. are convinced that the high standard of beauty which they desire to attain in Garden City can only result from simple, straightforward building, and from the use of good and harmonious materials. They desire as far as possible to discourage useless ornamentation, and to secure that buildings shall be suitably designed for their purpose and position.

All building designs were to be reviewed by company architects. Nevertheless, the company wanted to lease the sites with as little difficulty as possible, so they were not willing to contend with owners who had their own architects and wanted to build what they liked. As a result, the design controls were not strictly enforced.

Over time, the area of the town expanded. Today, Letchworth is an active community with a 2010 population of around 34,000. Local organizations include the Letchworth Garden City Heritage Foundation and the First Garden City Heritage Museum. The Letchworth Garden City Society meets in the building that once housed the Skittles Inn. Foundation Day is celebrated on Norton Common.

The buildings and open spaces of Letchworth make it possible for residents to develop an active social life. Parks, civic buildings, sports facilities, public halls, schools, shops, places of employment, and communal living groups allow residents to offer a wide range of social programs. These contribute to a sense of community and civic identity.

THE NEIGHBORHOOD UNIT FORMULA, 1928

While Ebenezer Howard saw the city as a network of separate but connected towns, Clarence Perry saw it as a pattern of separate but connected neighborhoods.[12] He thought of each neighborhood as a racially and socially homogeneous community (he uses the words *neighborhood* and *community* interchangeably), and he devised a formula for designing the *neighborhood unit*: a safe, quiet, and attractive urban environment for families with children.

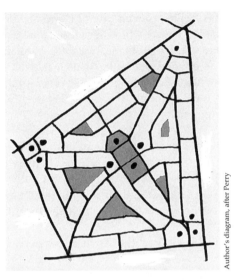

Figure 4.4. *Clarence Stein and Catherine Bauer write: "The neighborhood community is the basic unit of city building . . . The neighborhood shopping center . . . supplies the daily and staple needs of the homes within a limited radius . . . It gets little if any patronage from outside" (Stein and Bauer, "Store Buildings"). Elsewhere, Perry writes: "A place should be reserved for a church, provided it is known in advance that its parish is to be generally coterminous with the neighborhood" (Perry, "Neighborhood Unit Formula").*

Each neighborhood unit was to be more or less self-contained, with its own elementary school, church, parks, playgrounds, and civic buildings—facilities whose service areas would coincide with those of the neighborhood. A neighborhood would not be entirely self-sufficient. Police, fire, and utility services would remain the responsibility of the city. Residents would also rely on the city for employment, higher education, cultural activities, and major shopping. The size of a neighborhood unit would be determined by the service area of an elementary school, with the requirement that no pupil be more than a half hour's walk from home. This produced a unit size of 6,000 to 9,000 people.

Each unit was to be bordered by highways connecting with the interior streets at only a few points. The interior streets would provide circulation within the area but would be discontinuous to discourage through traffic and speeding. Shops on the bounding highways would make up a neighborhood shopping center that "differs from the regional or metropolitan market in that it depends on purely local trade."[13] All facilities in the neighborhood unit were also for the use of local residents.

Major civic and community buildings were placed around a central commons or square. Perry saw this as a formal place with "a flagpole, a memorial monument, a bandstand, or an ornamental fountain," and "suitable embellishments," such as ornamental arches and architectural markers. He envisioned residents going there for civic and religious activities. It would be a place where local celebrations would take place—where the flag would be raised and the Declaration of Independence recited on the Fourth of July. The center would be a visible sign of unity and a reflection of residential pride. It would increase the probability that residents would work together for the common good. "With . . . an environment possessing so much of interest and service to all the residents," Perry writes, "a vigorous local consciousness would be bound to arise and find expression in all sorts of agreeable and useful face-to-face associations."[14]

Perry also believed in the special importance of shared recreation facilities, and he writes that when "residents are brought together through the use of common recreational facilities, they come to know one another and friendly relations ensue."[15] This idea of the neighborhood as a self-serviced entity with an activity node as its geographic and symbolic center is a concept that has had a great influence on community design to this day. We see examples of its application in Radburn, New Jersey, and Seaside, Florida (discussed in chapter 2), as well as Celebration, Florida (discussed in chapter 3) and Columbia, Maryland (discussed next in this chapter).

There are, however, some questions about the relevance of the neighborhood unit formula today. Between 1946 and 1950, the neighborhood unit concept was applied in the first group of British new towns, J. E. Gibson notes.[16] Each town was planned as a series of neighborhoods, each with its own shops, primary school, community center, church, and so on. But the neighborhood failed to function as a cohesive unit, and so it was rejected as a basic planning element in the later towns.[17] I will note some of the problems with the formula in the discussion of the community of Columbia, Maryland.

COLUMBIA, MARYLAND, 1967

The city of Columbia is in Howard County, Maryland.[18] Alton J. Scavo, senior vice president of the Rouse Company, the developers of the town, says, "This is not a real estate project . . . it's a community development project."[19] Columbia was planned to accommodate 100,000 people and has successfully reached that goal.

The driving force behind the undertaking was James Rouse, who envisioned a community without racial or class segregation—a town that contributed "by its physical form, its institutions, and its operation to the growth of people."[20] Rouse assembled a multidisciplinary team known as the work group, made up of experts in the fields of family life, recreation, community structure, education, health, local administration, and communications. He asked the work group to define the optimum conditions for community life. Acting on his convictions and their suggestions, Rouse formulated a set of social goals, referred to variously as the Columbia Concept, the Columbia Process, and the Columbia Spirit, to guide the development of the town. These goals, adopted by the early residents and passed on to their successors, continue to shape public discourse in Columbia. Angela Paik, a reporter for the *Washington Post*, writes:

> Residents might not be able to define the "Columbia process," but they know what it is. It's tied to the town's 1960 roots and has something to do with having a close-knit, active community where residents of different races and backgrounds have voices that are heard, where people live in small villages and value open space and openness.[21]

Columbia attracted like-minded people by promoting the vision of an open-minded, color-blind, forward-looking society—a new America. The vision was planned and marketed, and it was used to guide development. James Rouse is said to have instructed realtors that once they had sold most of the houses on any one street to white families, they must offer the remaining houses to black buyers.

A pioneer resident of Columbia recalls that she had grown up in an area where "only the trash man [was black]. I did not want my kids to grow up thinking that only blacks were trash men. I couldn't deal with that, so we moved here." She adds, "People who are now adults that were born in Columbia and went to the school system and have gone outside of Columbia to live . . . have come back home in astonishing numbers because they find the rest of the world is not like this."

The first residents felt that they were responsible for laying the foundation for a new kind of society.[22] They are concerned now that later residents do not have the same level of commitment. One of the pioneers told me that Columbia "was not just a place to live, but a way of life. I know people who moved here, who came after we came . . . who moved here because it was a pretty place, not because it's got a sense of community and all these values that we were looking for." These views show that in order for a vision to endure, it must be constantly renewed.

A team of economists, mortgage bankers, real estate developers, and marketing and scheduling professionals began to set up religious, health, cultural, and educational programs, and at the same time, they worked with planners and designers on the physical plan. The plan shows the town as a cluster of 10 villages arranged around a downtown core. Each of the villages housed 10,000 to 15,000 residents and included three or four neighborhoods.[23] Each neighborhood had a mix of detached houses, town houses, and apartments. Houses in the same price range were grouped together, but the individual groupings were not so large as to encourage social isolation, and they were close enough to one another so that people of different lifestyles would use the same local facilities.

At the center of each neighborhood there was a swimming pool, an elementary school, a day care center, community meeting rooms, a park, playgrounds, and a small convenience store. At the center of each village, there was a secondary school, stores, doctors' offices, a library, and recreational and

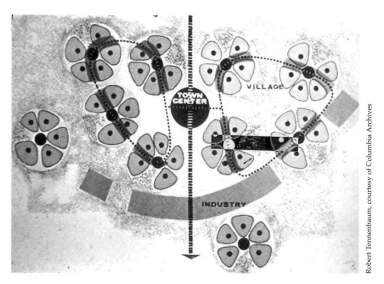

Figure 4.5. *This 1965 diagram illustrates the Columbia concept of neighborhoods, villages, and town.*

religious facilities. The town center was visible from the interstate highway and situated in the geographic center of the area. It consisted of a regional shopping mall with extensive parking, offices, and community buildings. A lake provided an attractive setting for restaurants, an inn, and a cinema. There were paths and plazas for leisurely recreation and public events.

The designers of the transportation network distinguished among through roads, neighborhood loops, cul-de-sacs, and walking paths. Through roads skirted the residential areas. A minibus system, running on a separate right-of-way, linked the village centers with the town center so that about a third of the population lived within a three-minute walk of a bus stop. (Unfortunately, the minibus system did not work out and was replaced by the county bus service.)

The planners believed that the division into neighborhoods and villages would facilitate interaction and generate local participation at different levels; that it would further sociability, civic action, professional and occupational growth, a feeling of interdependence, and a sense of common goals and common fate. The planners attempted to increase opportunities for meetings in the course of everyday arrivals and departures by clustering houses around cul-de-sacs and by having a number of housing units share a bank of mailboxes.

Fences were discouraged on the basis that they hindered interaction. (It is interesting to note that the designers of Seaside and Celebration, Florida, argue that fences encourage interaction.) Separate but related facilities were arranged so that people on different errands would meet and be encouraged to mix and interact. Schools were located so that children would be conveniently close to the facilities in the village center; and the school library, auditorium, pool, tennis courts, and playing fields were designed to be shared with the community.

Experience in Columbia has shown that there are problems with the concept of self-serviced neighborhoods and villages. First, the service areas of different facilities did not coincide with one another. For example, the area that was suitable for an elementary school was not necessarily a convenient size for a tot lot, nursery school, or convenience store. The idea of having a religious facility in each village center did not work out, because some denominations preferred, for reasons of economy and prestige, to have their own large, central building.

The composition of the neighborhoods also changed over time, with the result that some neighborhood schools became over- or undercapacity, some pools became overcrowded, and nursery schools had to be abandoned. The duplication of facilities in each neighborhood proved to be inefficient. Middle and high schools and major recreational facilities could not be duplicated at each village, and village-level libraries resulted in split collections.

Neighborhood stores had a hard time competing with big box outlets and supersize markets. They never became local hangouts, centers of information and gossip, as planners had expected they would, and it was hard to get people to run them because, as the director of community development for the Rouse Company put it, "Mom and pop wanted to run the 7-Eleven next to the Giant."[24] In the struggle to compete with larger chains, stores in the village centers began to serve specialized markets, drawing shoppers from other parts of town.[25]

Another problem came from the residents themselves. They recognized the neighborhood with its neighborhood center as a physical unit, acknowledging it as their address, but they did not necessarily see it as a social unit. Residents did not draw their friends from within the area's boundaries and did not necessarily socialize with their coresidents unless there was a local crisis.

Before the first resident moved in, the planners created the Columbia Association, or CA (formerly known as the Columbia Park and Recreation Association), a nonprofit corporation funded by user fees and a levy on the assessed value of property. The Columbia Association's function was to maintain all of the open spaces and to provide facilities and services for residents beyond those provided by the Rouse Company and the local government. The association's facilities included swimming pools, golf courses, an ice rink, a horse center, three lakes, extensive areas of parkland, and swim, athletic, and sports clubs. The developers appointed the first board of CA, but the long-term plan called for each village to have an elected village board, and each village board to have one representative on CA. As more villages were built and more residents moved in, the majority control of the board passed from the developers to the residents.

The Columbia Association distributes information about the history of the community and the purposes and responsibilities of membership. It sees itself as the custodian of the Columbia Spirit, as seen in its mission statement:

> The Columbia Association will endeavor to promote community in the sense that Columbia is a community whose members are aware of Columbia's purposes, are concerned for the welfare of each other as members of the community, welcome diversity of life styles and beliefs, deal constructively with conflict, and assume responsibility for the actions of the group.

These sentiments are repeated every year when residents get together to celebrate Columbia's birthday, although the Rouse Company has been replaced by General Growth Properties. Many provisions of the plan are being contested and have been amended, but residents still ask themselves what James Rouse would have wished before making important decisions.

Robert Tennenbaum, courtesy of Columbia Archives

Figure 4.6. *James Rouse cuts the cake at one of the annual birthday parties in Columbia, Maryland.*

LAKE CLAIRE COHOUSING, ATLANTA, 1977

Lake Claire Cohousing is located about three miles east of downtown Atlanta, in an established residential area known as Little Five Points.[26] Twelve town houses (with about 37 residents), a common house, and 24 parking spaces occupy a narrow, one-acre strip of land. The common house, which has a covered entrance porch, faces the street and serves the collective needs of the residents: There is a large social room, commercial kitchen, children's room, laundry room (the houses average 1,300 square feet, so many residents prefer to do without individual washing machines), bathroom, notice board, and individual mailboxes and cubbyholes.

The off-street side of the common house—the side that is used most often—opens onto a small courtyard with a paved patio, an outdoor fireplace, and a fountain. A passage connects the patio with the parking lot. A 10-foot-wide path runs from the courtyard, between two rows of town houses, and ends in a grassy area, which has a tree house and play equipment. Plants, arbors, plaques, wind chimes, and a fountain line the path, creating an engaging natural walkway. Several units are accessible from the grassy area, but most are accessed from the main path. The south-side units between the path and the parking lot have small patios or decks in the front, while the north-side units have patios at the back.

The design of Lake Claire Cohousing expresses the principles of social contact design endorsed by the cohousing movement, which started in Europe in the 1970s and began to take off in the United States 20 years later. Typically, members participate in the design of their community and make a commitment to share all management and programming responsibilities. They live in their own units and have joint ownership of the common spaces and the common house. Because residents use

Photo by the author

Figure 4.7. *In Lake Claire Cohousing, Atlanta, a 10-foot path provides access to all of the housing units and links them to the common house. Residents say that the closeness of the units and the narrowness of the path "eases," "nudges," or "forces" them into socializing with one another (residents quoted in Torres-Antonini, "Our Common House").*

Photo by the author

Figure 4.8. *The picture shows the main courtyard, outside the common house. Greg Ramsey, the architect and a resident of Lake Claire Cohousing, envisioned it as an outdoor room—an active community space to be used for storytelling, outdoor dining, dancing, theater and musical performances, and craft shows (Ramsey, quoted in Lindeman, "Designing for Small Spaces").*

shared facilities in the common house, the individual units can be small, with small kitchens.

In Lake Claire Cohousing, the houses are arranged so that they are close to one another and to the front path or sidewalk. Some homes have comfortable front porches or patios, making it easy for residents to greet passersby. The houses are grouped in clusters, which are small enough so that residents in each cluster can tell who belongs there and who does not. The path system is designed for pedestrian use: Automobiles are parked in shared lots or behind the houses. Entrances are oriented so that people walk past one another's homes on the way from their cars to their front doors, and a clear distinction is made between public and private spaces so that there is no doubt about who occupies each space. The whole community has a unified look.[27]

Lake Claire Cohousing was initiated by a group of people who became interested in the cohousing movement. They collaborated through the four years that it took to plan, finance, and construct the buildings. It follows that they were a self-selected set of people. They came prepared to participate in a communal lifestyle, which involved frequent meetings and extensive group discussions using conciliatory decision-making strategies to resolve differences of opinion.

Residents gather up to four times a week for communal meals. They organize group social and leisure activities, such as exercise and art classes. Each resident is expected to volunteer eight to 12 hours a month to work on community tasks, such as gardening or preparing shared meals, and in addition, to serve on one of the standing committees on landscaping, management of the common house, membership, and construction and maintenance. Families in the surrounding neighborhood participate in some of the activities in the common house, and Lake Claire Cohousing residents are members of the Lake Claire Community Land Trust, a neighborhood-based organization that created and maintains a two-acre park adjacent to the cohousing site.

A participant observation study of Lake Claire Cohousing found that the residents interact with one another on an almost daily basis.[28] They care about one another's welfare, assist one another in practical ways, and share goods and resources. "Less than a family but more than friends" is the way one resident describes it. The study attributes this strong sense of community to the fact that residents came in with a common vision. The study also finds that the narrowness of the pedestrian street and the need to circulate through it to get to the houses, parking lot, and common house force both desired and undesired interaction. Residents say that they consistently meet one another in the common house while preparing meals and eating together, engaging in leisure-time activities, attending meetings and social gatherings, collecting their mail, and using the laundry facilities. The close physical setting makes social contact inevitable; for residents who are less community minded, such closeness may produce conflict.

Lake Claire Cohousing is a case where the functionality and appearance of the setting and the selection, organization, and programming of residents are given equal weight. The physical and social plans are both directed at creating a community. Lake Claire Cohousing has this in common with the other examples in part 2: The community they create is not one that will suit everyone.

SUMMARY

The communities I reviewed in this chapter teach us different ways community facilities and services can be provided. In Riverside and Letchworth, the emphasis is on the provision of community-serving facilities (in the first, open space; and in the second, a town center). In Columbia and Lake Claire Cohousing also, the emphasis is on facility management and programming, and community participation. These four communities also have features I note in chapters 2 and 3: They were designed to attract similar people, create community organizations, and celebrate local traditions. Columbia is an especially instructive example of the application of all of these design features.

Columbia also teaches us that the idea of self-serviced neighborhoods, recommended in the neighborhood unit formula, does not fit with the way we live today and that neighborhood-based stores have a hard time competing in today's economy. (For further discussion of neighborhood stores, see chapter 8.)

We also see the recurrence of other community-generating design features. The communities in this chapter attract like-minded people. Lake Claire Cohousing attracts people who are interested in cohousing, Columbia appeals to liberals, Riverside is designed for "people of taste and refinement."[29] They cater to long-term residents, are concerned with physical form and appearance, and have clear boundaries. In Letchworth, the boundaries are established by a green belt; in the neighborhood unit, by highways; and in Lake Claire Cohousing they are implied by change in physical form and appearance. Riverside is an excellent example of another principle noted earlier: the use of design to bring people together through leisure-time activities. Riverside and Lake Claire Cohousing illustrate another use of the physical setting to generate community: The buildings and spaces are arranged in such a way that people are likely to meet by chance. Lake Claire Cohousing and Howard's original plan for the garden city are good examples (though less extreme than Twin Oaks, Virginia, discussed in chapter 2) of designs where individual residents stand to benefit directly from the successes of the community. All four communities have distinctive physical settings that reflect a collective identity. We saw this also in Carmel-by-the-Sea, California (artistic), and Celebration and Seaside, Florida (traditional).

It should be noted that facilities are generally associated with programs and activities. The Riverside plan calls for boating, skating, and picnicking in the public grounds; the neighborhood unit formula envisions public celebrations in the central square; Columbia offers activities in the town centers; and Lake Claire Cohousing has an eating-together program in the common house. Physical closeness does not necessarily make people socially close, so management and programming are important considerations in a community design.

CHAPTER 5

Ongoing Traditions and the Historical Past

Communities . . . have a history—in an important sense they are constituted by their past—and for this reason we can speak of a real community as a "community of memory," one that does not forget its past. In order not to forget that past, a community is involved in retelling its story.

—Robert Bellah et al.[1]

In this chapter, I discuss the role of shared history in binding people together. It may seem strange to discuss the value of shared history in new communities when that is the one thing the residents are sure to be lacking. However, each of the new communities in this chapter has a story about its history that residents find comfortable and interesting. Some of these stories are based on fact and some are built out of whole cloth. What is relevant here is that if residents accept the story, they will use it as the foundation of their collective identity. Santa Fe, New Mexico, and Chadds Ford, Pennsylvania, have sanitized and edited stories of their origins; Mariemont, Ohio, has a story of another place and time; and Opa-locka, Florida, has a story from *The Arabian Nights*. Themes and motifs from these stories are reflected in and reinforced by local architecture, parades, and festivals.

SANTA FE, NEW MEXICO, 1912

In 1880, the railroad bypassed Santa Fe, New Mexico, and the local economy began to decline.[2] The city government decided to use tourism as the key to its economic revival. They marketed the image of Santa Fe as a distinctive, historic town combining indigenous Indian and Spanish-style architecture. The Comprehensive Plan of 1912 noted that historical appearance was the town's "most priceless possession, an individuality which raises us above hundreds of other American Cities," and recommended that in the interest of "bringing about some sort of architectural homogeneity," no building permits be issued "until proper assurance is given that the architecture will conform exteriorially [sic] with the Santa Fe style." The planning board urged that "everything should be done to create a public sentiment so strong that the Santa Fe style will always predominate."[3]

The problem was that there was no existing Santa Fe style. In 1916, work began on the construction of a new fine arts museum, a picturesque composition combining elements from mission churches and Pueblo villages. A local historian noted, "Six of the ancient Franciscan mission churches, three hundred years old, are reproduced in its facades, without destroying the unity of its appearance."[4] Ironically, a number of historic adobe courtyard houses were demolished to make way for the new museum. The new building incorporated handcrafted, historically accurate details, mission-style furniture designed by the museum staff, and murals that traced the history of the town back to the city's patron saint, Francis of Assisi.

The New Mexico Museum of Art serves as an exemplar of the Santa Fe style, elements of which include long and low structures; irregular forms; uniform use of flat roofs; natural-colored adobe walls and buttresses; recessed portals; the absence of arches; casement windows; projecting tree-trunk roof beams,

Courtesy of Palace of the Governors (MNM/DCA), negative no. 022835

Figure 5.1. *The New Mexico Museum of Art, in Santa Fe, invented a traditional style of architecture out of "serviceable fragments from our regional, family, and ethnic traditions, mixed with borrowings from other times and peoples, and leavened by pure invention" (Wilson,* Myth of Santa Fe, *4).*

called *vigas*; roof drains, called *canales*; and ornamental roof brackets, called *zapatas*. Exterior porches, cloistered courts, balconies, balustrades, and towers relieved the solid appearance of the buildings. All of these architectural elements came from indigenous Pueblo and Spanish architecture, but Spanish-era baroque towers were rejected to avoid confusion with the California mission style. In this way, an expatriate community invented a new building tradition.

Architects began to experiment with the new idiom. Home interiors were furnished with Navajo blankets, Pueblo pottery, and New Mexico mission–style furniture. The chamber of commerce promoted Santa Fe as the "City Different."

The change in the appearance of the town was accompanied by a change in the composition of its population. Immediately following World War I, a group of intellectuals and artists, attracted by the "exotic" quality of New Mexico, settled in Santa Fe. Supported by the staff of the New Mexico Museum of Art, they embarked on a broad program of reviving Native American and Hispanic arts.

After World War II, the city's suburban subdivisions began to carry covenants limiting house builders to "the New-Old Santa Fe, Pueblo or Spanish style of architecture." In 1956, the *Santa Fe New Mexican* warned its readers: "Our chief danger lies in the fact that we are fast becoming less and less unique, and more and more like any southwestern community of comparable size."[5] The paper called for a design control ordinance that would require all buildings to conform to the Santa Fe style. In 1957, the city adopted an ordinance requiring that a "Historic Style Committee shall judge any proposed alteration or new structure for harmony with adjacent buildings, preservation of historic and characteristic qualities, and conformity to the Old Santa Fe Style."[6]

Almost yearly since 1911, the town has held a fiesta celebrating the town's colorful history, incorporating the processions, parades, pageants, and tableaux of the different religious,

Figure 5.2. Although the fiesta in Santa Fe, New Mexico, was initiated in 1911, it is promoted as a community tradition that goes back to 1712, when the Spanish governor, Diego de Vargas, celebrated his reconquest of Santa Fe from the Native Americans. This photo is from 1921.

ethnic, fraternal, and civic groups. The fiesta ignores the historical relations among the Spanish, Native American, and American populations, which were anything but friendly, and presents instead the image of a united, multicultural community. Once again, Santa Fe rewrites its history and uses the revised version to build a collective identity.

CHADDS FORD, PENNSYLVANIA, 1703

Chadds Ford is located in southeastern Pennsylvania, near Philadelphia.[7] Since the end of the 19th century it has been home to a number of artists, the most celebrated being the Wyeth family, painters of landscapes and rural life. In the 1950s, when suburbanites began to move into the Chadds Ford area, they saw the landscape as depicted in Andrew Wyeth's paintings, and guided by this vision, they developed the area to fit his image of undisturbed nature and agricultural land. The tradition of rugged individualism suggested in Wyeth's paintings was translated into a tradition of exclusivity and extreme privacy.

Residents purchased vacant land to keep it from being developed. They set houses well back from the road and used trees or several rows of corn to screen their carefully maintained lawns from public view. They included farm ponds in the open spaces and preserved decaying barns as picturesque elements. They designed houses in period style and garages that look like old Quaker horse sheds. Realtors sized up potential clients to determine if they were "Chadds Ford kind of people."[8] Local stores began to sell souvenirs based on Wyeth's paintings and postcards with low-angled shots of barns and countryside, carefully composed so as to cut out views of the adjacent highways, parking lots, and gas stations. The Brandywine River Museum started to display paintings by local artists, further reinforcing the area's unique character.

The new residents discovered that the area had a historical legacy as well: It had been settled by English Quakers in 1703 and was the site of the Revolutionary War Battle of Brandywine in 1777. They began to trace a continuous line between the significant events in the past—that is, events with which they identified and felt comfortable—and their own arrival in the area, and in this way they made the history of the area their own. The site of an old Indian settlement was preserved, streets were given Revolutionary War names, and Battlefield Park commemorated the Battle of Brandywine (most likely not on the actual battlefield, as that site had already been developed).[9] The community organized an annual Chadds Ford Day to commemorate the Battle of Brandywine. The Chadds Ford Historical Society purchased and restored old buildings and opened them to the public, and the Brandywine Conservancy fought to prevent further suburban encroachment on the pastoral area and to promote the causes of conservation and preservation.

By combining the vision of the area from Wyeth's paintings with the area's 18th-century history, the residents of Chadds Ford created a collective image of themselves as an artistic community living in a historic, picturesque, and rural

Photo by the author

Figure 5.3. *The Barn Visitors Center, headquarters of the Chadds Ford Historical Society. A notice in front of the center reads: "Designed to look like an 18th century Pennsylvania bank barn with two additions, the structure was actually built in 1990 on the footprint of William Hoffman's dairy barn." What you see only looks historic; what you don't see really is.*

Figure 5.4. *Chadds Ford Day is essentially an arts and crafts show, but the participants dress in costumes that portray 18th-century country life in the mid-Atlantic colonies.*

village—a place where life was settled, simple, and slow paced. This vision was promoted through marketing and advertising, and validated by its ability to attract tourists.

MARIEMONT, OHIO, 1922

Mrs. Mary Emery, a Cincinnati philanthropist, founded the town of Mariemont, Ohio, to house workers and pensioners of Emery Industries.[10] Charles Jacob Livingood, as Mrs. Emery's advisor and later as president of the Mariemont Company, was charged with implementing the project. He selected a 253-acre site (later expanded to 365 acres) on the main line of the Pennsylvania Railroad and hired John Nolen, a prominent planner of the day, to design the town.

Nolen's plan featured an octagonal-shaped town center and village green. All major civic buildings were located there. Seven roads radiated from the town center. Two roads ran to

the ends of the town and defined the edges of four neighborhoods, each with a school at the heart of its own small center;
two roads led to small business areas; a third led to a concourse
on the bluff overlooking the Little Miami River; and the fourth
road linked the town center with a number of parks and a
man-made lagoon. A section was set aside for pensioners' cottages and a home and workshop for convalescents. Eventually,
additional acreage was acquired for a hospital, golf course, and
industrial park.

Livingood was taken with the idea of recreating an English village. He commissioned 26 architectural firms to each
design a group of buildings that expressed the concept of an
English village. The "period" of each group was left to the
individual architects, with the result that different sections and
some streets within a section had a different style. For example, the dominant style of the center was English half-timber,
one residential area was Georgian colonial, and one street was
Elizabethan.

Local landscape architects created a different planting plan
for each neighborhood. Nolen wrote, "[The] greatest care has
been exercised to secure fine architectural design combined
with harmonious variety. The community picture will thus
be assured protection against the defacements that come from
indulgence in individual whims and the willfulness of bad
taste."[11] An interdenominational stone church was designed in
the Norman style, with 14th-century lichen-covered roof-stones
imported from England. Livingood reviewed all proposed
details. By the time the town was ready for occupancy in 1924,
it was too expensive for Mrs. Emery's workers and pensioners, and it became a white, middle-class suburb of Cincinnati
(restrictive covenants prevented sale or rental to blacks).

During the Great Depression, the town fell on hard times
(the vacancy rate in 1932 was as high as 40 percent), and construction came to a halt. Many of the public buildings and the
cottages for Emery pensioners envisioned in the plan were
never built. In 1931, the Mariemont Company was dissolved
and the management of the town was turned over to the nonprofit Emery Memorial foundation.

In 1942, the residents, who then numbered about 2,000,
voted to incorporate. They faced the question of their collective

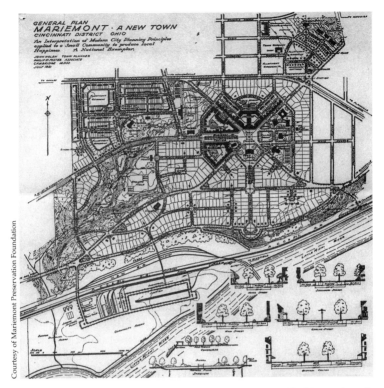

Figure 5.5. *The plan of Mariemont, Ohio, has many similarities to that of Letchworth, in the U.K. Nolen described it as a "convenient, practical and beautiful town" for a community of wage earners, with an initial population of about 5,000 people (quoted in Hancock, "John Nolen," 371).*

identity, and, taking a lead from the town's architecture, the residents agreed that they would present themselves as a small, old-fashioned English town. They created the position of town crier who had the job of ringing a hand bell to call the town meeting to order and introducing speakers. They also created the position of village marshal, the chief law enforcement officer, who wore a helmet like that of a bobby and a large star-shaped tin badge on his chest, and carried a large mace and a kerosene lantern. Zoning and building codes required all architecture, especially in the town center, to conform to the English

Ron Schroeder, courtesy of Mariemont Preservation Foundation

Figure 5.6. *Mariemont's appearance as an "old English village" was the basis for the community's identity. This is a photo of the Mariemont Inn.*

style. In 1967, the town acquired an authentic double-decker London Transport bus to take visitors around town.

At about the same time, it dawned on Mariemonters that their town had its own distinguished history: It was perhaps the first example of garden city planning in America. Residents then created the Mariemont Preservation Foundation and began to publicize and celebrate this history. In 1979, the National Park Service included Mariemont on the National Register of Historic Places, based on the town's garden city origins and its connection with John Nolen. (No mention was made of the town's more fanciful, constructed history.) Residents created an architectural review board to preserve the distinctive historical and architectural character of the area that contained most of the original buildings. Some new buildings, including a supermarket and a drive-through bank, also adhere to the Tudor- or Georgian-revival style.

Mariemont shows how the origin of a development can determine its future identity. The fact that Mariemonters were able to switch their origin story from "English village" to "historic site" suggests that it doesn't matter so much whether the story is real or made-up. The important thing is that residents accept it as their own.

OPA-LOCKA, FLORIDA, 1925

Opa-locka, located in Miami–Dade County, Florida, was created by Glenn Curtiss, a multimillionaire aviator and inventor, who had earlier developed nearby Hialeah, following a Spanish architectural theme, and Country Club Estates (now the city of Miami Springs), in the pueblo style.[12] Curtiss intended Opa-locka to be his dream city, a community where residents could live, work, grow their own food, and play. He wanted it to be distinctive enough to attract speculators from up north, so his architect, Bernhardt E. Muller, suggested a medieval English village with winding lanes, thatch-roofed cottages, and a castle with a tower and embattlements. Instead, Curtiss sent him a volume of *The One Thousand and One Tales from the Arabian Nights* with watercolor illustrations, telling him, "This is what I want Opa-locka to be like."[13] In December 1925, Curtiss formed the Opa-locka Company, and construction began early in 1926. Later that same year, with a population of less than 40 qualified voters, Opa-locka was granted a municipal charter.

The town was laid out by the urban planner Clinton McKenzie, with broad streets, avenues, and boulevards with names such as Aladdin, Sesame, Caliph, Ali Baba, and Sinbad.[14] Muller reviewed and approved all buildings to ensure conformity to the Arabic theme, and he designed more than 86 structures (many of which are still standing) incorporating elements of Islamic architecture, such as domes, minarets, horseshoe arches, crenellated parapets, distressed brickwork, rough-textured surfaces, and faded earth-tone colors. His drawings include details of "cracks" in the stucco, which exposed underlying areas where weathered bricks were inserted into a structure of reinforced masonry. His domes were hollow half spheres set on flat roofs. The focal point of the town was the administration building, a mosquelike structure with domes, minarets, and arches.

Many of the men employed in building Opa-locka purchased lots and moved there with their families. At the end of 1926, the town had attracted just under 300 residents from many different states. It included a school, firehouse, zoo, golf course, and swimming pool, as well as several churches and stores. The residents had formed a PTA, chamber of commerce, volunteer police force, hunt club, riding academy, and archery club.

Opa-locka was widely promoted as "the Bagdad of Dade County," making reference to Douglas Fairbanks's popular 1924 movie, *The Thief of Bagdad*, and the town quickly became a tourist attraction. Curtiss planned to add Egyptian, Chinese, and English sections, but development was halted in the late 1920s by a series of setbacks, including the Florida real estate crash in 1927, the onset of the Great Depression in 1929, and finally the death of Glenn Curtiss in 1930. Shortly before his death, Curtiss gave the United States Navy a piece of land for a small airfield, sparking the development of a naval reserve base, which expanded in 1939 into land that was to have been part of the city. When the base was decommissioned in 1960, an important part of the local economy went with it. Opa-locka became a low-income town, engulfed by the urban sprawl of Dade County.

In 1982, the Opa-locka City Hall was in a bad state of repair. There were plans to demolish the hall, but Opa-lockans rallied to its defense, and in 1987 it was completely restored. Unfortunately, in 2007 structural and sanitary conditions forced the city to abandon and board up the building.[15] Still, city leaders have capitalized on their community's unique architectural theme, and with help from the Dade Heritage Trust and the Florida

Courtesy of Florida Historical Society

Figure 5.7. *The Administration Building (until recently City Hall), at the intersection of Opa-locka and Sharazad Boulevards, in Opa-locka, Florida. Photo taken in 1926*

Figure 5.8. *In 1927, Glenn Curtiss invited a number of dignitaries to inaugurate the new railroad; residents of Opa-locka, Florida, rode out on horseback to meet the train, wearing Arabian costumes rented from a New York theatrical costumer.*

Trust for Historic Preservation, they ran a campaign to rescue some 75 structures built during the 1920s. Twenty-four buildings were placed on the National Register of Historic Places. Several new businesses have picked up on the Arabian motif. Every year the city organizes the Arabian Nights Festival to reinforce its origin story.

SUMMARY

The four histories in this chapter have design features I examined in chapters 2 through 4: They attract similar people, create community organizations, provide community facilities, cater to long-term residents, and have a unified appearance. Most notably, the histories in this chapter show how designers can use architecture and celebrations to remind residents of their (not necessarily accurate) common history, and even to make up their own origin story.

These histories also show some devices community designers use to suggest to incoming residents, who are complete strangers to one another, that they share the same history, background experiences, and values. Signs of age are fabricated to suggest continuity through time, as in Celebration, Florida (chapter 3). Architectural styles associated with generally known periods and places are used to create a familiar environment, as in Seaside, Florida (chapter 2). Annual celebrations, such as the Arabian Nights Festival in Opa-locka, fiesta in Santa Fe, and Chadds Ford Day in Chadds Ford, commemorate important events, bring residents together as members of a community, and, in turn, create their own traditions. Other examples are May Day in Twin Oaks, Virginia (chapter 2), the annual Bach Festival in Carmel-by-the-Sea, California (chapter 3), and the annual birthday party in Columbia, Maryland (chapter 4).

The four histories in this chapter also raise questions for community designers: Is it ethical to present a doctored version of the past rather than the real thing—the way a place would like to be seen rather than the way it is? These questions touch on larger concerns about the composition and appearance of a community, and how these affect community-relevant behavior. I will discuss these concerns further in chapter 6.

PART 3

Community Design

CHAPTER 6

The Appearance of Community

When we look at the most beautiful towns and cities of the past,
we are always impressed by a feeling that they are somehow
organic . . . Each of these towns grew as a whole, under its own
laws of wholeness . . . and we can feel this wholeness . . .
in every detail.

—Christopher Alexander[1]

As I see it, the purpose of community design is to generate community-relevant feelings and behaviors rather than create a work of art. Amos Rapoport, a leader in the field of environment-behavior studies, describes this approach as follows:

> The purpose of environmental design is not for its practitioners to express themselves "artistically." An "extreme" formulation of the consequences of this position is that designers' satisfaction should come from problem identification and solving. Designers . . . need to produce environments that they themselves may detest if they work for the users concerned . . . The products of such design (buildings and other physical environments) must be based on an understanding of human characteristics and must fit and be supportive of those . . . It follows that design must be based on knowledge of how people and

95

environments interact . . . design becomes the application of research-based knowledge.[2]

The designers of the developments described in part 2 (with the exception of Twin Oaks, Virginia) take a different approach. They see urban design as an art form that must be judged by artistic standards, using principles of structure, focus, sequential experience, meaning, and affect. Raymond Unwin, the designer of Letchworth, in the United Kingdom, believed that the principles of urban design "are simply [those] of architecture applied on an extended field."[3] Greg Ramsey, the designer of Lake Claire Cohousing, in Atlanta, is quoted as saying, "I think that the challenge of cohousing is to create . . . exciting transitions and thresholds."[4] Clarence Stein, the designer of Radburn, New Jersey, writes, "The planner's work is in many ways surprisingly like that of the skilled scenic designer."[5]

These designers are not insensitive to the effect of the environment on user behavior, but they see behavior as a consequence rather than an object of design, and they depend on intuition rather than research-based knowledge to go beyond appearances.[6] This is the artistic approach to design. Henry Moore, the famous English sculptor, explains this approach in relation to his work:

> In my sculpture, explanations often come afterwards. I do not make a sculpture to a program or because I have a particular idea I am trying to express. While working, I change parts because I do not like them, in such a way that I hope I am going to like them better. The kind of alteration I make is not thought out. I do not say to myself that this is too big or too small. I just look at it and, if I do not like it, I change it. I work from likes and dislikes and not from literary logic. Not by words, but being satisfied with form.[7]

Urban designers are necessarily more concerned about user needs than are sculptors, but they tend to follow a similar design process. Donald Schön refers to this as "reflective practice." Schön and Peter Rowe, in separate studies, have recorded how designers first imagine a solution to a problem, and then challenge and refine it through a series of sequential iterations.[8] When urban designers write about their work, they use the vocabulary of art rather than science—they talk about center, edge, hierarchy, unity, harmony, and composition. (See Figure 6.1.) They want their designs to "exhibit the same principles of design that any true work of art exhibits," and as illustrated in Figures 6.2–6.5, they apply the rules of artistic composition to the design of towns and neighborhoods.[9]

Figure 6.1. *In her painting* Planning a City, *South African artist Ruby Reeves comes down squarely on the side of the artistic approach to planning.*

A UNIFIED COMPOSITION

Boundaries

Figures 6.2a–c. Objects inside a common boundary appear to be different and separate from objects outside the boundary. *A bounding line in a painting separates figures into those inside and those outside the line. A theater proscenium separates a cast of actors from the audience and the everyday world. The green belt around Ebenezer Howard's garden city and the highways that ring Clarence Perry's neighborhood unit create a physical and visual separation between one development and another, and imply a social separation between one community and another.*

Courtesy of Lalit Kala Akademi, New Delhi

Figure 6.2a. Warli painting, Threshing the Paddy

Corbis Professional Licensing

Figure 6.2b. *Theater performance*

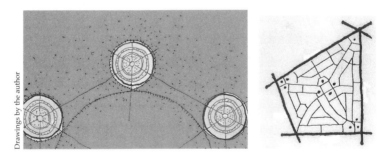

Drawings by the author

Figure 6.2c. *The garden city and neighborhood unit*

Hierarchical structure

Figures 6.3a–c. Objects are placed in a succession of ever-larger arrangements. *Small architectural elements in Salisbury Cathedral, in England, are combined to form successively larger ones. Planting beds in a formal garden are grouped and grouped again, each around its center. The arrangement of houses in Columbia, Maryland, clustered around cul-de-sacs, within neighborhoods, within villages, within the town, suggests that residents live in small communities but are still part of the larger community.*

Figure 6.3a. *Salisbury Cathedral, U.K.*

Figure 6.3b. *Planting beds in a formal garden*

Figure 6.3c. *Columbia, Maryland*

Central focus

Figures 6.4a–c. Objects are arranged in relation to a central point or axis; the geometry then sets up a force field, within which each object has its proper place. *In a tableau, the place and pose of each figure is determined by her relationship to the dominant central figure. At Drottningholm Palace, in Sweden, the arrangement of building and garden elements around a central axis makes the building the focus of an overall composition. In Seaside, Florida; Mariemont, Ohio; and Letchworth, U.K., major roads converging on the town center suggest that the physical center of the neighborhood is the social center of the community.*

Figure 6.4a. *Still from the movie* Million Dollar Mermaid

Photo by the author

Figure 6.4b. *Drottningholm Palace, Sweden*

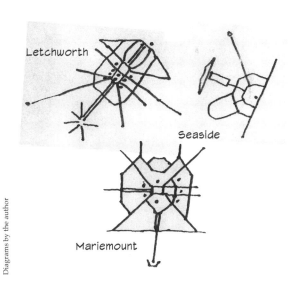

Diagrams by the author

Figure 6.4c. *Mariemont, Ohio; Seaside, Florida; and Letchworth, U.K.*

Conformity

Figures 6.5a–c. Objects that conform to a common theme appear to "go" together as members of a family. *Cheerleaders wear matching costumes to show that they are members of a team. Matching shapes and colors suggest that individual elements, while not identical, are part of an overall pattern. The matching stylistic elements of houses in Celebration, Florida, suggest that residents have similar tastes*

Figure 6.5a. *University of Wyoming cheerleaders, in the 1910s*

Figure 6.5b. *Huichol yarn painting*

Figure 6.5c. *Houses in Celebration, Florida*

The purpose of artistic composition, as illustrated here, is to make individual objects look as if they are elements of a larger whole. Clarence Stein writes:

> The unit of design in New Towns is . . . a whole community; a co-ordinated entity. This means that the framework of the community and every detail down to the last house and the view from the windows must be conceived, planned and built as a related part of a great setting.[10]

This is an aesthetic rather than social purpose.

Nevertheless, the appearance of wholeness, when applied to a community design, reads as an expression of cooperation and like-mindedness. Buildings that defer to one another seem to be related to one another and look as if each is a part of a larger whole; and we transfer the idea of relationship from the buildings to the people associated with them. The appearance of wholeness is the appearance of community. The appearance of wholeness is often combined with a design theme to suggest that this is a special kind of community and prospective residents are buying not just a house but a way of life.[11] A theme is often reinforced by slogans and advertisements—for instance, in Seaside, Florida, "The New Town. The Old Ways." Celebration,

Courtesy of Mariemont Preservation Foundation

Figure 6.6. *Mariemont, Ohio, has a town crier who wears a white wig, red velvet jacket, black brocade waistcoat, black velvet breeches, and custom-made shoe buckles forged by the blacksmith at Colonial Williamsburg, Virginia.*

Florida, describes itself as "A new American town of block parties and Fourth of July parades. Of spaghetti dinners and school bake sales, lollipops, and fireflies in a jar."[12] It is in response to a design theme that the town crier in Mariemont, Ohio, dresses in wig and breeches, while residents in Chadds Ford, Pennsylvania, dress as colonials; in Santa Fe, New Mexico, as conquistadores; and in Opa-locka, Florida, as belly dancers.

A COMMON THEME

One may ask why people are willing to accept a theme set by a developer (especially a theme that is as patently phony as "The Bagdad of Dade County") as the basis for their collective identity. Glynis Breakwell suggests that it is because people look for relationships that confirm their feelings of uniqueness, continuity over time, and personal and social worth.[13] It follows that if a theme proclaims a place as the home of a distinctive, prestigious, and enduring community, people will want to be associated with it and be part of it. In a time when so many localities are indistinguishable from one another, a strong identity, even if it is borrowed, is preferable to anonymity. Even if the theme is quirky, being quirky is better than being ordinary, and a make-believe pedigree is more desirable than none at all.

The ability of a theme to express a collective identity is especially evident when existing communities decide to reinvent themselves. Following are four examples.

Litchfield, Connecticut, 1913

In 1913, the residents of Litchfield, Connecticut, decided to "restore" their town to fit the popular image of a New England colonial town. In actuality, many of the houses had been built in the 19th-century Victorian style, the surviving 18th-century houses had not been built in the colonial style, and the only houses that were originally built as "colonials" were 20th-century additions. In order to accomplish the restoration, some houses were altered beyond recognition.

In the 1980s, the Litchfield Historical Society changed the colors of two of their buildings, arguing that early American structures had not all been white with green shutters, but townspeople objected. A member of the board of burgesses is

Courtesy of Litchfield Historical Society

Figure 6.7. *The Fitzgerald-Hickox house in Litchfield, Connecticut, sometime before 1913*

Courtesy of Litchfield Historical Society

Figure 6.8. *The Fitzgerald-Hickox house in Litchfield, Connecticut, in 1997, restyled to fit the image of a colonial town*

reported to have complained, "Historical accuracy can be carried too far." Today, the town is listed on the National Register of Historic Places, even though the "historical" past the buildings represent is fictional.[14]

Frankenmuth, Michigan, 1854

The town of Frankenmuth lies in the Saginaw valley, about 80 miles north of Detroit.[15] It was settled in 1845 by a group of 15 immigrants from the province of Middle Franconia, in Bavaria, who had come to do missionary work among the Native Americans. Friends and relatives from Franconia came to join the colony, and in 1854 the Township of Frankenmuth was created. By 1858, there were approximately 1,000 inhabitants, two schools, two churches, two stores, a post office, a hotel, a grist mill, two sawmills, and several blacksmiths and wagon shops. By 1875, there were 25 businesses, including a brewery and a sausage maker. Frankenmuth was incorporated in 1908. Today,

Courtesy of Frankenmuth Historical Association/Museum

Figure 6.9. *The first Bavarian Folk Festival was organized by the Frankenmuth Bavarian Inn; today it is an annual event and is run by the town of Frankenmuth, Michigan.*

the residents of Frankenmuth retain many of their early German observances and customs.

In 1959, the owners of the former Fischer's Hotel remodeled it and reopened as the Frankenmuth Bavarian Inn, adding a new dining room in the Bavarian style of architecture, with traditional German food served by waiters in lederhosen and waitresses in dirndls. To celebrate their heritage, they organized the Bavarian Folk Festival, which evolved into the annual Bavarian Festival.

One after another, Frankenmuth merchants bought into the theme and built or remodeled their buildings to mimic the timber-framed buildings of Franconia, with decorative half-timbering, high-pitched roofs, deep overhangs, and towers. *German Life* describes the town as follows:

> Main Street is lined with shops in Alpine-style architecture. Banners supporting the blue-and-white Bavarian flag hang on every light pole. Local restaurants are famous for serving good food, and beer is still brewed locally. There's a chapel replicating a famous one in Austria's Tyrol and a Glockenspiel that tells a Brothers Grimm tale on the hour. The calendar is packed year 'round with events including an Octoberfest, Volksläufe and Snowfest.[16]

In 1963, the Civic Events Council of Frankenmuth took over the operation of the Bavarian Festival, which draws between 80,000 and 100,000 people each year. Today, Frankenmuth is promoted as "Michigan's Little Bavaria."

Mount Airy, North Carolina, 1960s

Mount Airy, North Carolina, was the inspiration for the fictional town of Mayberry in television's *Andy Griffith Show*, which ran from 1960 through 1968. Now tourists can visit Floyd's Barber Shop, Wally's Service Station, and Aunt Bee's Room, all named after characters in the show. The City of Mount Airy and the Surry Arts Council host the annual Mayberry Days Parade featuring character look-alikes. Souvenir shops on Main Street sell Mayberry shirts, mugs, and key chains. The

Courtesy of Hobart Jones/Surry Arts Council

Figure 6.10. *The Mayberry Days Parade in Mount Airy, North Carolina, in 2005 included Elizabeth MacRae, who played Betty Parker in episode 217 of* The Andy Griffith Show.

town has a promotional video in which a Barney Fife impersonator (Barney Fife was the fictional character played by Don Knotts) describes the "authentic small-town experience." An ex-resident comments that "Mount Airy, a real town, wants to present itself as Mayberry, a fictional town, and to help it do so, it's hired an impersonator to play an actor who played a TV character."[18]

Stockbridge, Massachusetts, 1967

For a few days each Christmastime, the residents of Stockbridge, Massachusetts, change Main Street to reproduce the 1967 painting that Norman Rockwell made of it for the cover of *McCall's Magazine*. A Stockbridge resident observed that the painting "epitomizes what we want a small town to be."[17] The town closes the street; residents bring in vintage cars, decorate

Figure 6.11. *Norman Rockwell's painting* Home for Christmas *(Stockbridge Main Street at Christmas) appeared in* McCall's Magazine, *December 1967.*

Courtesy of Stockbridge Chamber of Commerce

Figure 6.12. *Every year at Christmastime, Stockbridge, Massachusetts, recreates itself in the image of Rockwell's main street.*

the street fronts, and place candles in the windows; and a band plays World War II–era music.

SUMMARY

In this chapter we saw that a unified and expressive physical design can result in a place and a community becoming known by the same name; they will be connected in people's minds so that like-minded residents will be attracted to move there, new residents will be encouraged to behave in community-relevant ways, and outsiders will see and treat all residents as a group.

It bothers me that a designer can decide a community's identity before the first resident even moves in.[19] While the history of Opa-locka, Florida (see chapter 5), suggests that even the most bizarre theme may find acceptance by at least the first generation of residents, there is a danger that in later years it will be a false façade, a Potemkin village.[20] Lake Claire Cohousing, Atlanta (see chapter 4), offers one solution to the problem, which is to have residents participate in the original design. In Carmel-by-the-Sea, California (see chapter 3), the designer proposes a theme, and the residents complete it. In Mount Airy (this chapter), residents recreate themselves by introducing a new theme.

Designers should be careful not to confuse the appearance of community with the real thing.[21] Community appearance by itself is no more than a stage set. It fosters relationships only when it serves as a catalyst for collective action. For this reason, considerations of appearance should be accompanied by considerations of the other community-generating characteristics that I have identified, such as like-minded people (chapter 2), local organizations (chapter 3), and ongoing traditions (chapter 5).

To create these characteristics, community designers must rely on both knowledge and intuition. When designers are required to represent the interests of populations that are outside their personal experience—people of different age, sex, income, or class, or with different backgrounds, expectations, and customs—research-based knowledge is the more reliable of those two options. However, research is incomplete and limited to questions that are researchable; beyond that, designers must rely on educated hunches. Even if, one day, research-based knowledge is complete, the success of a neighborhood design will still depend on the artistry with which knowledge is assembled and applied.

CHAPTER 7

Community-Generating Neighborhoods

There really can be no other right purpose of community except to provide an environment and an opportunity to develop better people. The most successful community would be that which contributed the most by its physical form, its institutions, and its operation to the growth of people.

—James Rouse[1]

Until now, I have tried to identify neighborhood properties that generate community. In part 1, I looked to see what I could learn from research in the social sciences, and in part 2 to see what I could learn from designers of new planned communities and from the experience of people who live in these communities. I learned three things. They are:

- Certain neighborhood properties serve to generate community; they can be introduced through design.
- Not everyone wants to live in a close-knit community.
- Some communities serve the interests of the larger society better than others.

TEN PROPERTIES OF A COMMUNITY-GENERATING NEIGHBORHOOD

What follows is a list of the properties of a community-generating neighborhood. Some are solidly supported by research, while others stem from an intuitive reading of actual community designs. They are not listed in any order of priority, although I suspect that the first four are the most important.

1. It attracts people who are predisposed to getting along with one another.

This is perhaps the best single predictor of community. People who share the same values and lifestyle are likely to meet and interact even in the most unpromising environments. Chances of interaction are increased if, in addition, the design projects an image that attracts community-minded residents, and incoming residents understand that they are expected to participate in community activities. Designers use advertising, sales practices, pricing, and symbols associated with certain groups or values to target particular populations and to steer away or screen out those who are felt to be incompatible. These measures can raise important ethical questions and should be used with caution.

2. It has community organizations that serve as vehicles for collective action.

Local organizations offer opportunities for people to come together and work on matters of common concern. They make it possible for a group to speak with a single voice. Communities of like-minded residents are likely to create these organizations by themselves with little or no outside support, although preestablished organizations will help speed up the community-building process. Mixed income and mixed tenure communities are far more likely to depend on design intervention in the initial stages of their development.

3. It includes facilities such as stores, parks, plazas, and civic buildings that bring people together under conditions that are conducive to meeting and interacting.
Neighborhood facilities are gathering places, but with the ease of automobile travel and the proliferation of choices, the people who gather there may not consist entirely, or indeed at all, of residents from that neighborhood. This suggests the idea of facility-based rather than neighborhood-based communities. Chances of interaction are increased when the facilities attract regular users and invite leisure-time activities. Opportunities for interaction are increased when a variety of facilities are clustered together in a center or a main street. Neighborhood stores, because they serve everyday needs and are open to all, are thought of as "public" facilities—more public, for example, than schools, museums, and city offices.[2] There is evidence to suggest that small independent stores are more community minded than large-scale retailers.[3]

4. It triggers residents' collective memory.
A landscape reflects the times and circumstances of its creation. It is a repository of meanings. By "reading" the landscape, people are reminded of memories that they share and that bind them together as a community. These memories are commemorated in familiar settings, meaningful buildings, monuments, and place-names. They originate in and are renewed by special events, participation in local activities, the repetition of local stories and myths (some designs go so far as to invent these), and annual festivals and parades. How do we read a themed landscape such as that of Opa-locka, Florida? What does it tell us about its designers or about its residents? Does it trivialize the language of architecture, or does it take advantage of its vocabulary? These are questions that designers must ask themselves.

5. It is a suitable size for a neighborhood-based community organization.
If a residential area is too big, it may be difficult for all residents to come together as a single community; but if it is too small, it may be ineffective in influencing areawide policies.

Photos by the author

Figures 7.1a and b. *Annual celebrations and rituals hold communities together and remind them of their common roots, like these dolls in the Museum of International Folk Art, Santa Fe, New Mexico.*

Larger areas can be created by clustering several neighborhoods under a single umbrella organization. Smaller areas can be created by dividing sections of the city into separate sectors or quarters. But one cannot assume, as Léon Krier does, that an appropriately sized geographic division will become "the built expression of a community."[4] Appropriate size is, I suggest, a community-generating property, but it is not enough. It is only effective as one of a package of the properties listed here.

6. Its houses, spaces, and related uses are arranged in such a way as to facilitate social interaction among residents.

Opportunities for casual meeting are greater when houses are closer to one another and to the road; domestic activities are brought out of the house onto front porches and into yards; groups of residents use the same path to reach their front doors; and these doors are visible from other houses. Increasing the frequency of meetings increases opportunities for interaction. Unfortunately, it increases opportunities for both friendly and unfriendly interactions, and so the effectiveness of this property is tied to the presence of other community-generating properties I have mentioned, mainly those of attracting like-minded residents and forming community organizations.

7. It creates conditions under which individual residents stand to benefit from the success of and lose from the failure of the collective.

Individuals are most likely to participate in a community if it is in their self-interest to do so—especially if the value and quality of their homes are directly affected by changes in the neighborhood. In some communities—for example, those associated with condominiums, cooperative housing, and cohousing—residents share a fiscal interest in the common spaces and the legal right to manage internal changes. Other community organizations provide a platform for individuals to influence outside forces that threaten the neighborhood—for example, zoning regulations, property assessments, and traffic management. Communities with greater mutual dependency have a greater need for cooperation, and this may be a problem in situations where residents lack the will or experience to engage in cooperative work.

8. It encourages leisure-time use.

People who are at leisure are more likely to interact because they have time to socialize and also because leisure-time activities tend to be seen as play, evoking a sense of camaraderie.[5] Residents who spend their leisure time in the neighborhood are more likely to interact with their neighbors.

A resident of Columbia, Maryland, told me: "Columbia has always had both people in a household going out to work, so it's a suburban desert in the daytime . . . people tend to come home late . . . once they make dinner, they take care of their kids' club activities, then they will hole up."[6] Residents are more likely to interact in a meaningful way if they meet in a park instead of the workplace or while attending to chores. Shady sidewalks, as well as parks, swimming pools, libraries, and recreation centers—and programs at these facilities— attract leisure-time users.

9. It caters mostly to long-term residents.

Long-term residents tend to have a greater financial and social investment in a neighborhood—they know more people, are more willing to participate in local events, and have a greater sense of community. John Nolen, the designer of Mariemont, Ohio, writes, "Only in settled communities where a sense of personal responsibility among the people prevails can a genuine social life manifest itself."[7] Neighborhoods are more likely to generate community if they cater to home owners rather than to renters.

10. It has the appearance of community.

A unified composition does more than serve purely aesthetic purposes. It has the appearance of like-mindedness, and residents are tempted to live up to appearances. Visual motifs and distinctive elements are seen as expressions of community identity. Creating the appearance of community should not, however, take the place of building a real one. Appearance is only effective in combination with other community-generating properties; alone, it simply creates a stage setting.

I have several comments about the 10 properties as a whole. First, they support one another, in the sense that each is at the same time a means and an end. For example, people who get along are more likely to develop shared memories, and people who have shared memories are more likely to get along.

Second, some properties have direct implications for the composition and arrangement of the physical environment, while others refer more directly to development, sales, and management practices. Together, the properties confirm that a community-generating neighborhood is a combination of neighborhood-as-place and neighborhood-as-locus-of-community. They draw upon a number of disciplines, and more than one community-building property is required to ensure a successful community design.

Third, properties that serve to generate a community may not be needed to sustain it once it is established and has developed its own history and culture. I look back to communities examined in part 2: Levittown, New York, and Radburn, New Jersey, no longer exclude certain groups of residents; Carmel-by-the-Sea, California, no longer offers a subsidy to artists; and Roland Park, Baltimore, no longer draws its residents from the social register.

Fourth, some neighborhoods, such as Locust Point, in Baltimore, acquire community-generating properties through the action of market forces or through self-selection. Residents in these neighborhoods form communities with little or no outside intervention. In neighborhoods that have few or weak community-generating properties, such as some mixed use projects, the need for outside intervention is especially urgent. (See the study of HOPE VI projects in chapter 8.)

And finally, certain properties that are essential for one type of community may be marginal or irrelevant for another; therefore, the 10 properties can be assembled in different combinations to create different types of community. To illustrate this point, let us imagine four community types.

FOUR TYPES OF COMMUNITY

There is no ideal community. Some people look to their neighbors for friendship and support, some prefer to be left alone, while others fall somewhere in between. If designers are to design for community, they need to know what type of community to design for. Here, a community typology comes in useful.

Think of a typology as a number of bins, with each bin standing for a type of community. One sorts communities into these bins so that the properties in one bin are more alike than those in any other bin. A type is a distillation of the properties in a single bin. It is not a description of a real community; real communities generally fall between bins.

My community typology consists of four types: tribal communities, communities of convenience, floating communities, and asocial communities.[8] Thinking back to the histories in part 2, Twin Oaks, Virginia, comes closest to the tribal, and Rosebank comes closest to the asocial type. Most of the others are communities of convenience. There are no floating communities in part 2 because I chose only communities with active organizations. Floating communities are to be found in center cities, college campuses, cruise ships, and summer camps.

Tribal Community
A tribal community is a close-knit community with a high level of social interaction and cooperation. Residents care about and confide in one another. They have long-standing relationships and overlapping friendship networks in which everyone knows about everyone else, their families, and their reputations. Ideally, a tribal community design should attract similar people, create organizations to bring them together, encourage home ownership, and provide a full complement of local retail, employment, religious, educational, and entertainment services. It should celebrate local history and traditions, have well-defined boundaries, and create an overall appearance that is distinctive and that reinforces group identity.

Community of Convenience
In this type of community, relationships are amiable rather than intimate and tend to be based on organizational connections

rather than personal contacts. Relationships are fragile: When problems arise, residents are inclined to move away rather than work things out. Ideally, a design for a community of convenience should attract residents with similar lifestyles and values, reducing the chances of conflict and the need for mediation. It should set up formal organizations that bring residents together on issues that threaten the quality of their shared environment, and it should also create a unified appearance that shows residents and outsiders the extent of the community area.

Floating Community

This is a community whose members are constantly changing. Individuals find themselves living among strangers for limited periods of time, and they look for friendships that are new and do not require long-term commitments.[9] Ideally, a design for a floating community should ensure a ready supply of rental housing at different price levels and provide facilities where it is easy to meet people (such as cafés and bookstores) and activities (such as events and get-togethers) that facilitate chance meetings and interactions. Efforts to screen residents are not needed, nor are attempts to develop formal organizations or to create a unified appearance.

Asocial Community

This kind of community is based on coexistence rather than cooperation. It attracts people who prefer to keep their neighbors at a certain social distance but may have a latent sense of community and will cooperate when their common interests are threatened. Ideally, a design for this kind of community should create a place with a distinctive character and history, where residents are allowed to act in parallel, rather than required to act collectively; can avoid social contact; and do not have to belong to anything. People do not have to be like-minded, there is no need for a strong community organization, and facilities and programs aimed at bringing people together are undesirable.

A design for any one of these neighborhood types can have unintended consequences. It can, for example, generate a form of association in which members identify with their neighborhood at the expense of society as a whole.[10] It can create selfish, protective, and exclusionary forms of association.[11] We need to design good communities of each type.

If, as I have suggested, communities are more likely to happen in community-generating neighborhoods, then it is reasonable to believe that good communities are more likely to happen in good neighborhoods—that is, neighborhoods that support local community building and, at the same time, are consistent with broad societal values.

FIVE QUALITIES OF A GOOD COMMUNITY DESIGN

James Rouse, the developer of Columbia, Maryland, describes a good community as one that has a diverse population, wide participation in community affairs, and a feeling of collective responsibility, security, comfort, and importance. It is a community that promotes individual and community health, provides a learning environment for children and adults, and is a good place in which to grow old.[12] Roland Warren defines a good community as one in which residents have a large measure of local autonomy and are able to deal with one another on a personal basis; there is widespread participation in community affairs; there is a wide variety of income, ethnic, religious, and interest groups; and there is a broad distribution of power.[13]

To come up with my own list of qualities of a good neighborhood, I have borrowed from Rouse and Warren, and from Kevin Lynch's "performance dimensions," which he describes in his seminal book, *A Theory of Good City Form*. In the end, the list represents my personal values.

Congruence
There should be a reasonably close fit between the physical form and appearance of a neighborhood and the way that its residents use it and think about it. Places that are visually prominent should also be socially significant; focal points in the composition should coincide with centers of community life; historical references should be meaningful to the residents; and things should look like what they are. We see examples of

congruence in places where key civic uses are located on important sites and housed in signature buildings. For example, this quality is present in the villages in Columbia, Maryland, where each subdivision is represented by a village center and serves both as an address and as a voting district for the Columbia Association.[14]

Self-determination

The neighborhood should represent the interests of its residents rather than those of its designers. A community organization should do more than perpetuate the original design: The organization should evolve to meet changing needs and circumstances. The development histories in part 2 offer examples ranging from communities where almost everything can be changed by the residents (Twin Oaks, Virginia), to those where almost nothing can be changed without the approval of the designers (Celebration and Seaside, Florida). Designs should be malleable enough to carry the imprint of community-defining events as they occur. Community organizations should be empowered to embrace new values and revise or renew old ones. Elements that give the design its overall coherence should be the slowest and hardest to change.

Inclusiveness

A neighborhood should not exclude people on the basis of race, age, sexual preference, income, or ethnic background. The selection procedures based on race and religion in Mariemont, Ohio; Radburn, New Jersey; and Levittown, New York, do not satisfy this requirement. The screening procedures practiced in cohousing developments do, however, because they are designed to include anyone who chooses a certain way of life. This strategy does not contradict that of attracting like-minded people if like-mindedness is understood to mean shared values. Nor does it preclude residents' desire to live with others similar to themselves, as long as homogeneous enclaves are small enough so that different enclaves share the same facilities.

Connection

Neighborhood facilities should be open to use by outsiders, without neighborhood residents necessarily losing local control, and neighborhood residents should be encouraged to use outside facilities but should not unreasonably compete with them. An example is the community of Lake Claire Cohousing, Atlanta, which invites outside residents to participate in activities in the common house, and also participates in running an areawide park. Rosebank, Baltimore, on the other hand, is an example of a community that restricts the use of its facilities to its own residents. Twin Oaks community, in Virginia, is virtually self-sufficient and runs the risk of weakening residents' ties with the outside.

Suitability

While working on this book, I am leading a graduate-level course on community design. Most students arrive convinced that a strong residential community is a good thing—it requires no justification. As they discuss the histories of different communities, however, they have second thoughts. Are they willing to accept the level of commitment and interdependency required in Lake Claire Cohousing, Atlanta, and even more so in Twin Oaks, Virginia? Is Rosebank, Baltimore, really a community? It becomes clear that different people balance their need for community and privacy in different ways.[15] Members of most residential communities share an interest in the value, quality, and security of their homes, but beyond that, some people prefer to live among neighbors who offer little more than civil behavior and cooperation in times of crisis, while others look for neighbors who share a wide range of interests and offer companionship and a sense of togetherness. A community design should aim for a place on the community–privacy continuum that suits its members.

All this talk about design may give the impression that it can accomplish more than it really can. Even if we create environments that are conducive to the creation of community, there are many variables that are beyond the designer's control. These include outside factors—such as changes in the economy, housing standards, and the composition of residents—and local factors, such as residents' desire for interaction.

CHAPTER 8

Policy, Management, and Process

We have also come to understand that, alone, [design techniques] are insufficient. Policy and management can work hand-in-hand with design to ensure results or, likewise, can conspire to make such results impossible.
—Andrés Duany, Elizabeth Plater-Zyberk, and Jeff Speck[1]

Participation is an education into public, shared, social life. It transforms dependent, private individuals into . . . people of a community.
—Robert Fowler[2]

The properties and values discussed in chapter 7 present a number of contradictions. For example, Seaside, Florida, teaches us to plan for neighborhood stores because they are places where residents meet and talk, but Columbia, Maryland, teaches us that neighborhood stores are closing because they cannot compete with the malls. Radburn, New Jersey, teaches us that like-minded people are the ones most likely to form a community, but I have said that a community plan should be inclusive and cater to people who are different. Levittown, New York, teaches us that residents do not need help from designers to organize themselves around common interests, but Rosebank, Baltimore, teaches us that common interests are not necessarily a catalyst for collective action.

In this chapter, I report on studies that address these three contradictions: A study of neighborhood stores suggests conditions under which the stores can be viable; a study of mixed income housing suggests conditions under which people in different income groups are likely to work together; and a study of participatory planning shows how the process of planning can lead to the formation of a community.

STUDY 1: THE NEIGHBORHOOD STORE

Many community plans call for neighborhood stores, but a Baltimore study, described here, suggests that stores may not survive without special protection, and this must be a concern of plans.[3]

Architects and urban designers have argued that community plans should include neighborhood stores because the stores facilitate social interaction and produce a sense of belonging.[4] However, can neighborhood stores really be economically viable in an age of malls, supermarkets, and bargain outlets? A Baltimore study explored this question by looking at neighborhood stores in Canton, an older Baltimore row-house neighborhood located across the harbor from Locust Point.

The Canton stores were originally located on street corners. Today, some of the corner properties have been converted to houses, and some of the row houses in between are used as stores, hairdressers, bars, offices, fitness centers, and the like, typically with residences upstairs. Locally, all of these small, scattered commercial uses are known as "corner stores," and I will refer to them by this name, even though they are not necessarily stores and not necessarily on corners.

The study asks how the stores originally came to the neighborhood and how they are making out today. It also asks how present-day residents, unaccustomed to living in a mixed use area, feel about corner stores—a question raised by a report that a group of residents in an adjacent neighborhood, Fells Point, was pressing to get corner stores off their streets: "A task force . . . has decided that the jumble must go. It has created a map that draws a line between residential and commercial, keeping homes next to homes, stores next to stores."[5]

The story of the corner stores begins in 1828, when the Canton Company acquired the land that is now Canton. The company built railroads and sold land for industrial uses, such as copper smelting, shipbuilding, iron refining, dye manufacturing, and oil refining, which attracted skilled workers from Wales, Germany, Ireland, and Poland. Some of the industries provided houses for their workers, but private builders erected most of the houses, on land purchased or leased from the Canton Company. These homes were known as row houses, a form that had existed

Photos by Rachel Fitzgerald

Figure 8.1. *Some of the corner stores in Canton, Baltimore*

in Boston and Philadelphia since the early to mid-18th century. They were economical to build and maintain, and affordable for industrial workers. The area was on the outskirts of the city, so the builders included stores at each street corner. This was a typical urban pattern in Baltimore at the time.[6]

The industries in Canton thrived until the end of World War II. In the 1950s, however, two things happened that would have a direct impact on the corner stores. First, the industrial plants began to close, and many of the younger residents moved to the suburbs. Second, with increased car ownership and the rise of shopping centers in outlying areas, Canton residents began to shop farther from home, lured by greater variety and cheaper prices. With a declining population becoming less dependent on the neighborhood, many corner stores closed.

The 1980s saw a new interest in waterfront living. Until then, Canton had housed a solidly working-class population, but the people now moving in were mainly professionals—younger, more educated, and wealthier. By the 1990s, the newcomers were rehabilitating the old row houses, stripping them of their Formstone facings and adding roof decks; converting industrial buildings to condominiums; and building new town houses and apartment buildings. New marinas lined the shore, and property values and housing prices soared.

The number of corner stores continued to decline, but at a diminishing rate. Some of the remaining stores were converted to housing; some continued to serve the thinning number of old-time residents; some repositioned themselves to attract the new residents; and some reinvented themselves as coffee or wine shops, bookstores, art galleries, and health centers. A 2005 survey showed 158 corner stores remaining in Canton.

In order to understand the decline of the corner stores, one must understand the drastic changes that have taken place in the delivery of retail services since the time that the stores were built. It was a time when residents walked to the store, which provided a clear advantage to merchants who were located close to their customers. There was little need for advertising, as goods virtually sold themselves: Bread was bread; milk was milk.

Circumstances changed as mass production and mass marketing brought a huge increase in the number and diversity of goods. This, combined with increased ease of transportation, led to new forms of retailing. Prominent among these new forms were supermarkets and mass merchandisers, which took advantage of high car ownership and low land costs in outlying areas to build large-area facilities serving regional markets. Small stores could not carry the range of merchandise that newer, larger stores could, and because smaller stores did not have high enough sales volumes to qualify for manufacturers' discounts, they could not compete on the basis of price.[7]

Of course, price is not the only factor influencing a consumer's shopping preference. Many shoppers are prepared to pay a higher price in return for a more pleasurable shopping experience, and retailers have responded by providing settings that are attractive and exciting, or homey and restful.[8] Small stores cannot generally afford the kind of space, organization, and capital required for these amenities. In short, neighborhood stores are no longer a necessity, and a neighborhood location no longer guarantees local patronage.

The Canton study has two parts: interviews with owners and managers of 16 corner stores, and a questionnaire completed by 44 residents in Canton and the immediately adjacent neighborhoods. A word of caution is appropriate here. In a study of four San Francisco neighborhoods, residents reported a higher sense of community when the commercial uses were concentrated on a "Main Street" than when they were scattered.[9] For this reason, community plans that include neighborhood stores should see the Canton findings as a warning (results to watch for) rather than a prescription (a do/do-not design mandate).

Canton residents say that the corner stores are convenient, are especially important for elderly people, encourage walking and reduce the need for driving, increase neighborliness, keep the area alive, and help the tax base. One respondent calls them a basic ingredient of city living. In addition, they help to establish a community identity. They are places where people meet.

Storekeepers say that they feel part of the community and that they feel safe because their neighbors watch out for them. The manager of a home mortgage company says that she likes living among her customers because her building has the same issues their houses have. Several storekeepers speak about the

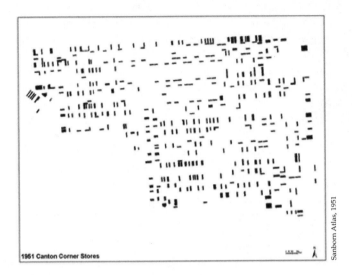

Figures 8.2a–c. *A comparison of the Sanborn Atlas of 1951 with University of Maryland surveys in 1989 and 2005 illustrates the gradual but steady loss of corner stores in Canton, Baltimore, over a half century.*

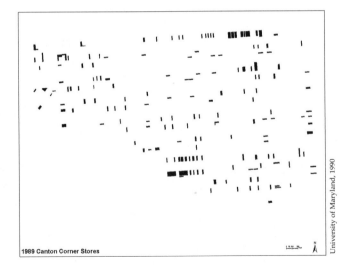

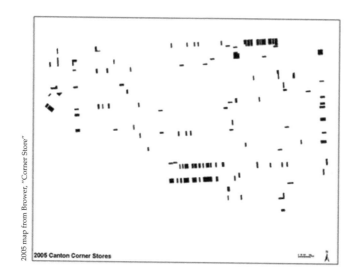

2005 map from Brower, "Corner Store"

2005 Canton Corner Stores

need to be solicitous of their neighbors and to "tailor one's business accordingly." One speaks about the importance of participating with the neighbors in keeping the street clean, because "it is the right thing to do." Many feel residents benefit from their presence. One storekeeper notes that her neighbors come in to use her coffeemaker, copier, and fax machine.

A number of storekeepers are involved in the community on a personal level as well. They contribute to schools and churches; give talks to local groups; and donate toys, food, cash, and gift certificates during the holidays and merchandise, such as coffee and donuts, for local meetings. Some stores offer credit to local residents; some receive packages and messages for their neighbors. (Parcels ordered over the Internet may be delivered during the daytime hours when residents are at work, so some people arrange to have them left at the corner store.) The stores provide employment for residents, and they advertise in the local papers. One storekeeper says that a business should "contribute back to the community" and that "you should spend your money where you earn it."

Coexistence does have some problems. Residents do not like all types of stores equally. Residents prefer stores that serve their daily needs and provide useful, needed, and perhaps unique services. Storekeepers find parking to be a problem, especially for stores that are open in the evenings and on weekends, when most residents are home. Neighbors complain about parking, traffic, trash, blaring music, and departing customers who are loud and uncivil. Most of these complaints are directed at bars and restaurants. They take the form of verbal communications, written notes, and in one instance, I was told, a court case (which the residents lost).

Many of the corner stores are marginal businesses and have a hard time competing with newer, bigger, upscale stores and chains in and adjacent to the area. Storekeepers report that the opening of a Safeway supermarket in the neighborhood caused four or five corner groceries to close down. The local hardware store no longer carries electrical appliances because it cannot compete with the discount stores, and the television repair store has fewer customers because most people do not want to spend money to repair a television when Walmart sells new sets so cheaply. Storekeepers are concerned about chains moving into the area. They are also concerned that they are classified as nonconforming uses in a residential zone, which means that most changes are tied up in red tape. These restrictions make the corner stores less competitive.

Storekeepers use a number of strategies in order to survive. Some run their stores with help from family members, who sometimes collect salaries and sometimes do not. Some storekeepers do not depend on the business as their sole source of income—some are retired, and some have other investments or depend on the outside income of a husband, wife, partner, or child. Some storekeepers own their building, or the building belongs to a family member, and so the storekeeper pays only token rent. Some live over the store or rent out the upstairs, a practice that has become more profitable as rents in the area have increased.

Certain storekeepers are pessimistic about their future. With rising real estate values, their properties are worth more than their businesses, and they feel that if they were to close, the buildings' uses would convert to housing. Other storekeepers are optimistic: They believe that small businesses will never disappear entirely, because people always want places that have a "family feel."[10] According to the storekeepers, businesses that stand the best chance of survival are convenience stores, restaurants, professional offices, and specialty shops not found in malls (general retail is not included in these categories).

The Canton study confirms that neighborhood stores contribute to the creation or strengthening of community and finds that residents will accept a mix of uses—but under certain conditions. A community plan with small stores should include a process for screening out stores that do not meet residents' criteria for good neighbors. These criteria refer to appearance (stores must be attractive and inviting, unobtrusive, blend in with the neighborhood, and have clear and uncluttered signage) as well as management (stores must be well run, respectable, and managed by "good people"—preferably local residents). Plans should consider including programs to train and motivate small merchants to become more competitive with mass marketers. Competitive strategies include offering the kinds of services and products that are not found in a typical shopping mall; working through buying groups to get trade discounts; providing clean, well-maintained, attractive, and welcoming premises; and doing what they do best—stressing personal attention.[11]

In addition, plans should build in a protective cushion against ruinous competition from chains and superstores. A number of cities faced with this concern have enacted zoning ordinances for residential districts that permit only stores that serve primarily local residents, prohibit or discourage large stores, and exclude chain stores.[12] The ordinances regulate the hours of operation and deliveries, signage, and exterior improvements of small stores, and the stores' potential impact on the surrounding neighborhood.

The fact that many cities have taken steps to encourage and protect small independent stores suggests that the findings of the Canton study have general relevance for community design.

STUDY 2: MIXED INCOME COMMUNITIES

A study of three mixed income developments in Baltimore shows that there are obstacles to social interaction between

lower- and upper-income residents, and suggests ways to overcome these obstacles.[13]

In many cities in the United States, old public housing projects are being demolished and replaced by mixed income
developments. The intention is to change the pattern of segregated neighborhoods—a pattern that leaves low-income
residents socially isolated and economically disadvantaged,
without "the mainstream role models that help keep alive the
perception that education is meaningful, that steady employment is a viable alternative to welfare, and that family stability
is the norm not the exception."[14]

By having residents of different classes live in the same
neighborhood, planners hope that low-income residents will
be able to benefit from increased social control, middle-income
role models, and more effective local leadership.[15] Mixed
income is a stated principle of the new urbanism movement,
whose charter states: "Within neighborhoods, a broad range
of housing types and price levels can bring people of diverse
ages, races, and incomes into daily interaction, strengthening
the personal and civic bonds essential to an authentic community."[16] Mixed income is also a goal of the federal HOPE VI
housing program.[17]

The HOPE VI program ("HOPE" is an acronym for Housing Opportunities for People Everywhere) was created in 1992
as a result of the National Commission on Severely Distressed
Public Housing. While the aims of the program have varied
somewhat over time, a consistent goal has been to create neighborhoods that combine subsidized and market-rate units so
that people from different socioeconomic backgrounds can live
together as a community. The three HOPE VI developments in
this study were all built in the same time period, between 2003
and 2005. They differ in their overall sizes, the percentage of
rental to ownership units, and the number and nature of amenities available to residents.[18]

The rental units at each site are owned and managed by a
private developer and, with a few exceptions, are occupied by
public housing tenants. The home owner units are sold on the
open market. In two of the developments, the for-sale units
are scattered, while in the third, they are off to one side. All
three developments are designed so that from the outside, a

passerby cannot distinguish between home owner and rental units (although residents recognize telltale signs, such as screen doors on the home owner units). Each site has a community building with meeting rooms, classrooms, and a kitchen, although the buildings differ in size, accommodation, and operation between the three sites.

At all three sites in the study, in-depth interviews were conducted with representatives of the Housing Authority of Baltimore City and the developers, and with community leaders, leaders of neighborhood associations, and specialists in the field of mixed income housing. In addition, at all three sites researchers used residential questionnaires and discussed their findings and preliminary conclusions with the residents. The questionnaires at each site were designed and administered by separate teams, but they covered the same ground (definition of *community*, residential history, neighborhood characteristics,

Photos by the author

Figures 8.3a–c. *In all three projects in the study of mixed income developments in Baltimore, the houses are designed so that owner and rental units cannot be distinguished one from other. The unified architecture masks a divided population.*

Figure 8.3b.

Figure 8.3c.

perceptions of renters and owners, effect of mixed income, civic engagement, housing management, and demographics) and included many of the same questions, some structured and some open-ended. At each site, members of the team went door-to-door. In most cases they filled in the forms, although in a few instances residents preferred to complete the forms themselves. In all, a total of 90 questionnaires were completed, representing 41 owners and 49 renters.

The findings show that owners and renters are satisfied with their houses and with the overall appearance of the developments, with renters somewhat more satisfied than owners. There is a good deal of interaction among the renters, especially those who lived together in the public housing projects that had previously stood on the sites (interestingly, some felt that there had been a greater sense of community in the project), but there is little interaction among the owners, who have activities and interests outside the housing area and are not committed to long-term residency. Public housing tenants and home owners share certain basic values and quality-of-life concerns—notably safety, maintenance, and sanitation—but these tend to be overshadowed by lifestyle differences, and each group holds stereotypical views of the other. There is virtually no interaction between owners and renters.

These findings should come as no surprise to those familiar with earlier work on mixed income (sometimes referred to as "balanced") communities. For example, Herbert Gans writes that heterogeneity at the block level "is unlikely to produce relationships of sufficient intensity to achieve either a positive social life or the cultural, political, and educational values sought through the balanced community." Amos Rapoport argues that perceptions of heterogeneity are based on lifestyle differences, such as attitudes to child rearing, food habits, and time-use patterns (rather than on demographic variables such as religion, class, race, education, and occupation), and that at the block level, these differences make life less predictable and reduce the chances of agreement and mutual support.[19]

The residents in the Baltimore study differ with respect to both income and tenure. If community is to be a goal of HOPE VI (which, it should be noted, residents in the Baltimore survey did not feel at all strongly about), then the plan should aim at creating settings that are especially favorable to the construction of community. The study reveals, however, the presence of design elements that do not encourage or that actively discourage interaction. These can be summarized under four headings: community organization, unequal responsibilities, shared facilities, and incentives.

Community Organization

Each development called for the creation of a residents association to represent both home owners and public housing tenants. One of the sites had a so-called Resident Association, but it consisted of home owners and just one tenant representative; according to the survey, the tenants felt that they had no say in the association's activities. In the other two sites, residents associations never materialized. Instead, the housing authority set up a tenant council to represent the public housing residents, and the developers set up one or more condominium associations to represent the home owners. There were no organizations that represented both groups, and there were no organizations dedicated to community building.

One may argue that organizations in mixed developments evolve slowly and that the Baltimore surveys were taken too early to see full evidence of a true community, but the conditions of the program are not encouraging. Studies of homogeneous housing developments have shown that organizations form almost as soon as the residents move in.[20] In a heterogeneous population, one can anticipate the need for an organization that will correct the stereotypes each group holds of the other and will identify, develop, and address common concerns, mediate in disputes, and create reasons and opportunities for residents to come together. The problems associated with the HOPE VI sites are particularly challenging because the heterogeneous population includes an engineered mix of people with both income and tenure differences. It is a great deal to ask of residents that they get together and organize themselves to meet these challenges, and to expect that they will succeed without sustained outside help.

Unequal Responsibilities

The units are designed so that ownership and rental units are visually indistinguishable. But the outward appearance of equality masks inequalities in the rights and responsibilities of each group, and this contributes to a certain amount of confusion and resentment. For example, the owners buy their units with few strings attached, while renters are required to sign a lease agreement that covers personal behavior as well as the upkeep of their unit (one that I saw ran to 52 pages in length). Renters can be evicted for not following the rules, but owners cannot. There is also the matter of property maintenance. The developers, who retained ownership of the rental buildings, hired a management company for their properties, and the home owners hired a management company for their properties. Sometimes these were different companies with different contractual responsibilities, so that, for example, a home owner might be expected to cut the grass in front of her house, while her neighbor, a renter who paid only nominal rent, had her grass cut for her. The inequalities between what appeared on the surface to be similar types of housing were more obvious in the two sites where the rental units were interspersed among the ownership units.

Shared Facilities

All three developments include a mix of incomes, but none incorporates a mix of uses. None includes public facilities or stores. Some residents use churches and stores in the larger neighborhood. However, although home owners were more likely than tenants to say they were part of the larger neighborhood (tenants were more likely to associate themselves with only their development), they were less likely to attend local churches or shop in the neighborhood stores. Home owners were also less likely to use neighborhood parks or schools because they were mainly young couples and empty nesters.

Children in the developments belonged to the tenants and were often a source of conflict. One of the developments had a small park, but it was operated and maintained by the home owners association as a place for quiet relaxation, despite tenants' frequent complaints that there was no place for their children to play. The community buildings, on the other hand, were run by or for the benefit of the tenants. Owners sometimes held meetings there, but only with the permission of the Tenant Council. This meant that there were few places that served both owners and renters by providing meeting grounds and creating opportunities for interaction.

Incentives

In all three developments, there were few incentives for home owners and renters to interact or work together. The housing authority saw the project as public housing and maintained contact with the tenants, mainly through the management company, but had nothing to do with the home owners. The developers marketed the for-sale units as good value for money. They did not attempt to attract community-minded people, and once the units were sold, the home owners were on their own. Some home owners were not even aware when they bought their houses that they were to be part of a mixed income community.

This study teaches us (by omission) that plans for creating mixed income communities must include certain key ingredients.[21]

First, every effort should be made to build on interests that the two groups have in common and to narrow the gap that divides home owners and tenants. The most obvious common interests come from living in the same place, which suggests that activities such as crime-watch and cleanup programs or competitions for the best-looking or most improved mixed income blocks would be beneficial to all parties. An obvious point of division between owners and renters is the incentive to make physical improvements. Owners stand to gain from improvements that increase property values; tenants do not, and additionally, they have to undergo regular management inspections. This suggests the need for creative forms of tenure that will reduce renters' dependence on outside management and give them rights and responsibilities that are closer to those of home owners. Examples include providing rent-to-buy units and making it possible for renters to benefit financially if they make improvements, such as adding screen doors, and engage in maintenance activities, such as cutting the grass.

Developers should market their developments as more than housing—instead, as a way of life. They should try to attract buyers who are community minded through targeted marketing and by arranging for prospective buyers to be informed about community goals and objectives. They should try to narrow the gap between groups of residents by attracting home owners who have children and consequently are more likely to share interests with the renters. This means that arrangements must be made for good neighborhood schools, day care programs, and supervised play areas. Another way to narrow the gap is to plan for rental-only or ownership-only units in a single development, while varying the size and cost of the units. This would separate income-mix from owner-renter differences. Finally, the developers should ensure that there are local facilities—such as food stores, parks, and playgrounds—where HOPE VI residents can meet with one another and with residents of the larger community. Some of these could be located within the development and others in adjoining neighborhoods.

The developers or the housing authority should set up a residents association that will create opportunities and reasons for owners and tenants to come together. The association should have broad representation and sufficient resources, and authorities should give it guidance and support until it is established and self-sustaining. It should have built-in procedures for arriving at consensus and mediating disputes. Programs could include a community newsletter to keep residents informed about local activities and interests, and a "welcome wagon" to greet new residents to the community.[22] It is not enough to create programs that cater to low-income residents. Middle-income residents will not participate in community-building processes unless they feel that it is in their interest to do so.

It is not clear from the interviews that residents in mixed income housing areas really want to get together as a community; but if this is desirable for larger societal purposes, then the Baltimore study suggests the importance of a setting that increases opportunities for forming a community. It may not be a community of friendships and intimate social ties, but at least it can be one that is based on mutual respect, cooperation, and the elimination of mistaken stereotypes.

STUDY 3: THE PLANNING PROCESS AS A GENERATOR OF COMMUNITY

Residents may have common interests, but these interests may not bring them together. Resident participation in planning Patterson Park, Baltimore, shows that the planning process can bring residents together and that the process, rather than the plan, can generate community.[23]

Patterson Park is in east Baltimore, approximately one mile from the inner harbor. It was established in 1827, when William Patterson, a Baltimore merchant (whose daughter, Elizabeth, married Jérôme Bonaparte, brother of Napoleon), donated six acres of land for a "public walk." A series of subsequent purchases enlarged the park to its present size of 155 acres. Today, the park is located in the center of a group of traditional Baltimore row-house neighborhoods. The neighborhoods differ considerably in their social and economic makeup, and each has its own community association.

In December 1993, the Southeast Planning Council, a coalition of more than 50 southeast Baltimore community leaders, recommended that the city should improve the parks in the area. Earlier that same year, planning students at the University of Maryland had conducted a series of interviews and observations in Patterson Park to find out how local residents feel about and use it.[24] The study found that the park is well used from early morning until late evening. Many local residents grew up around the park, and they have fond memories and strong emotional ties to it. Some use the park as an extension of their home and think of it as part of their neighborhood. However, others do not use the park at all because they associate it with drug users, prostitutes, and vandals. One respondent said, "The park is a battleground between those who want to make the city a better place and . . . those who don't care."

In 1995, the city undertook to prepare a master plan for Patterson Park. University of Maryland faculty and students worked with planners in the Baltimore City Department of Recreation and Parks (I will refer to this group of planners as "we") to involve local residents in the preparation of the plan.[25] The plan document itself was to be developed by consultants.

We undertook a series of structured observations in the park at different times of the day, on weekend days and weekdays to see who was using the park, when, and where. We found that the highest-use period was mid- to late afternoon; the count went up somewhat on the weekend. We also conducted telephone interviews with 229 residents who lived in the neighborhoods around the park. Seventy-eight percent of those who use the park say there are problems: They cite uncivil behavior of some users, fear of dogs, crime, and the poor condition of the facilities and grounds.

We called a general meeting of residents in the neighborhoods around the park. The participants established five standing committees. The Promotions, Marketing, and Management committee eventually absorbed the others, and it continued to meet until the completion of the master plan, in 1998. The landscape architecture firm of Rhodeside & Harwell prepared the plan documents, after meeting with the residents to listen to local interests and concerns and present their own concepts and proposals.[26]

At that stage, the members of the Promotions, Marketing, and Management committee transformed themselves into the Friends of Patterson Park ("the Friends"). They incorporated, acquired an office in one of the park buildings, and secured grants to hire a director and permanent staff, make capital improvements, and run programs. They adopted the slogan "Patterson Park: The best backyard in Baltimore."

We wanted to know whether residents felt that their involvement over a period of almost three years had been meaningful and whether it had produced the hoped-for benefits. In a series of interviews and focus-group meetings, residents told us that their participation was worthwhile, in large part because it gave them an increased sense of ownership in the park and responsibility for it. They felt the community shared in the ownership of the plan, and they were determined to see that the city carried it out.[27]

It is worth noting that individual residents had used the park before they got involved in planning, but the process of planning made them a community of users.

Ten years later, in 2008, faculty and staff of the university conducted a follow-up study in Patterson Park.[28] By this time, a number of the plan recommendations had been implemented, and in addition, the neighborhoods around the park were in the process of being gentrified. The average resident was now whiter, younger, wealthier, and better educated, and had fewer children than in 1995. Many of the houses had been renovated.

We repeated the series of observations in the park and received 440 responses to an online questionnaire aimed at residents who live around the park.

Our findings show that prostitution, crime, and drugs are still a problem, but people think the park is safer during the daytime, better maintained, and more welcoming than it was in 1995. Dogs are less of a problem. Residents use the park frequently, in all seasons, for a wide range of activities. The park is the reason why some people live there and why some do not leave. The Friends, often in partnership with other nonprofit organizations, have assumed much of the maintenance work and all of the programming responsibilities in the park. They involve residents in activities such as clearing the lake, repairing the structures, cleaning up, planting and mulching the trees, caring for the flower beds, and working on special events, such as summer concerts and the popular annual lantern parade.

Brower and Hislop, "User Survey of Patterson Park"

Figure 8.4. *Cumulative count of people observed in Patterson Park, Baltimore, on an average weekend day in the fall of 2007. Each dot represents one person. Counts were made at 1:30 and 10:30 in the morning, and 1:30 and 4:30 in the afternoon.*

Ninety-four percent of the respondents in our study said that they are familiar with the Friends, 42 percent are members, and 34 percent participate in activities organized by the Friends.

While residents recognize that the city has made significant improvements in the park, they give most of the credit for the park's success to the Friends. One responded, "Thank you so much to the Friends of Patterson Park for all of their hard work! You guys do a FANTASTIC [*sic*] job." Another said, "I think the changes in the community and Patterson Park in the seventeen years I've been in the neighborhood are remarkable. The improvements are great. Thank you so much."[29]

In short, the community of park users has survived and become more effective. The Friends have taken on the task of planning for the future of the park.

SUMMARY

The three studies in this chapter address some apparent contradictions in and between the principles and goals of community

Nkechi Hislop

Figure 8.5. *Asked if community participation in the plan for Patterson Park, Baltimore, was worthwhile, a resident replied, "When people are invested and involved, then they begin to feel ownership and begin to place a value on it. Once they begin to place a value on it they will take care of it" (Brower and Todd, "Community Participation in the Plan," 15).*

design. The study of a mixed income area shows that residents have little incentive to get together, but suggests that this can be overcome with appropriate organization and management. The corner store study shows that neighborhood stores contribute to a sense of community, but suggests that public policies are needed for their economic survival. The park study shows that common interests may not by themselves lead to community, and suggests that the planning process can harness this interest and serve as a platform for building community.

The studies show that a plan must consider the conditions necessary for it to be implemented. Talen makes this point in discussing the designs for rebuilding 11 towns along the Mississippi Gulf Coast that had been destroyed by Hurricane Katrina.[30] The designers wanted to create diverse communities with local goods and services within walking distance, and for that purpose they included a range of housing types, a mix of residential and nonresidential uses, and public spaces that would facilitate social engagement. But the designs were not implemented, because while the designers addressed changes in the traditional physical features of the towns, they did not take into account the prevailing politics and customs.

The three studies in chapter 8 affirm the conclusions reached in this book: A community design must apply community-generating principles, introduce a process for arriving at the appropriate application of these principles, and introduce policies and management practices that are needed for the applications to succeed. Plans, policies, and operations are the elements of a community design. Design has its limitations; however, I have tried to show that it can contribute to the creation of new communities and help strengthen existing ones. In emerging and changing areas, it can jump-start the community-building process and put residents on the path to constructing a collective identity.

NOTES

A NOTE TO THE READER

1. Stephanie McCrummen, "Redefining Property Values," *Washington Post*, April 18, 2006, A01.
2. See Dorit Fromm, *Collaborative Communities: Cohousing, Central Living, and Other New Forms of Housing with Shared Facilities* (New York: Van Nostrand Reinhold, 1991); Peter Katz, *The New Urbanism: Toward an Architecture of Community* (New York: McGraw-Hill, 1994); Evan McKenzie, *Privatopia: Homeowners Associations and the Rise of Residential Private Government* (New Haven, Conn.: Yale University Press, 1994); and Edward J. Blakely and Mary Gail Snyder, *Fortress America: Gated Communities in the United States* (Washington, D.C.: Brookings Institution Press, 1997).
3. Ralph B. Taylor and Sidney Brower, coprincipal investigators, and Steven Pardue, project director, "Longitudinal Effects of Crime and Signs of Disorder on Communities" (study, report submitted to the National Institute of Justice, Washington, D.C., 1995).

INTRODUCTION

1. Community Planning Studio, "Locust Point: Toward a Community Plan" (studio report, College Park, Md.: Urban Studies and Planning Program, University of Maryland, 2002). The residents were responding in 2001 to a survey question: "What makes this neighborhood special?"
2. Information about Locust Point comes from my personal observations and conversations with local residents and resident historians Jim Neill and Oleg Panczenko, Locust Point, 2001 and 2002; and from interviews conducted by my students in the Urban Studies and Planning Program at the University of Maryland in 2001 (URSP 708) and again in 2002 (URSP 607). Community Planning Studio, "Locust Point."

3. Michael Scarcella, "Locust Point Fire Kills Woman, 82, and Her Son," *Baltimore Sun*, December 12, 2001, 1B.

4. Interview with Joyce Bauerly, then president of LPCA, Locust Point, 2002.

5. Mayberry is the name of the warm and friendly fictitious community portrayed in *The Andy Griffith Show*, a popular sitcom that was aired on CBS from 1960 to 1968.

6. Thomas Bender, *Community and Social Change in America* (Baltimore: Johns Hopkins University Press, 1982), 7.

7. Corinne McLaughlin and Gordon Davidson, *Builders of the Dawn: Community Lifestyles in a Changing World* (Shutesbury, Mass.: Sirius Publishing, 1986), 10.

8. Kingsley Davis, *Human Society* (New York: Macmillan, 1949), 312.

9. Willis A. Sutton, Jr., and Jiri Kolaja, "Elements of Community Action," *Social Forces* 38, no. 4 (May 1960): 325–31.

10. Roland L. Warren, *The Community in America* (Chicago: Rand McNally, 1963), 9.

11. Gordon Rattray Taylor, *Rethink: A Paraprimitive Solution* (New York: E. P. Dutton, 1971), 108.

12. Ralph Keyes, *We, The Lonely People: Searching for Community* (New York: Harper and Row, 1973), 14.

13. Ralph B. Taylor and Sidney Brower, coprincipal investigators, and Steven Pardue, project director, "Longitudinal Effects of Crime and Signs of Disorder on Communities" (study, report submitted to the National Institute of Justice, Washington, D.C., 1995).

14. Ernest L. Boyer and Lee D. Mitgang, *Building Community: A New Future for Architectural Education and Practice* (Princeton, N.J.: Carnegie Foundation for the Advancement of Teaching, 1996), 148; Todd W. Bressi, "Planning the American Dream," in *The New Urbanism: Toward an Architecture of Community*, ed. Peter Katz (New York: McGraw-Hill, 1994), xxv–xlii.

15. Caplow, Stryker, and Wallace write: "The planner is excused . . . from planning the social details of good neighborhoods. We need only provide adequate physical facilities, both inside and outside the individual dwelling, and the society need only provide a rising level of welfare, for increased neighborliness to follow of itself." Theodore Caplow, Sheldon Stryker, and Samuel E. Wallace, *The Urban Ambience* (Totowa, N.J.: Bedminster Press, 1964), 168.

16. James W. Rouse, "It Can Happen Here" (speech, University of California, Berkeley, September 23, 1963). Available in the Columbia Archives, RG I, Series V, Box 4, Folder 3, Columbia, Md.

17. Jonathan Barnett, *Redesigning Cities: Principles, Practice, Implementation* (Chicago: APA Planners Press, 2003), 95; Henry Sanoff, *Community Participation Methods in Design and Planning* (New York: John Wiley, 2000). See also Arthur W. Mehrhoff, *Community Design: A Team Approach to Dynamic Community Systems* (Thousand Oaks, Calif.: Sage, 1999).

18. Eduardo E. Lozano, *Community Design and the Culture of Cities: The Crossroad and the Wall* (New York: Cambridge University Press, 1990), 35; Kevin Lynch, *A Theory of Good City Form* (Cambridge, Mass.: MIT Press, 1981), 48.

CHAPTER 1

1. Italo Calvino, *Invisible Cities* (New York: Harcourt Brace Jovanovich, 1974), 76.

2. These differences are discussed in Jeremy Boissevain, *Friends of Friends* (Oxford: Basil Blackwell, 1974).

3. The finding that living in the same area is not a necessary condition for community supports general experience: We all know communities whose members live in different parts of the city, the country, and even the world—think of Boy Scout troops, book clubs, religious congregations, fraternal societies, professional associations, and perhaps Internet chat groups and newsgroups. See Starr Roxanne Hiltz and Murray Turoff, *The Network Nation: Human Communication via Computer* (Reading, Mass.: Addison-Wesley, 1978); and Anita Blanchard, "Virtual Behavior Settings: An Application of Behavior Setting Theories to Virtual Communities," *Journal of Computer-Mediated Communications* 9, no. 2 (January 2004), available at http://jcmc.indiana.edu/vol9/issue2/blanchard.html.

   McClenahan identifies certain groups as "communalities," which are composed of people who meet on a regular basis, but not always in the same place. See Bessie Averne McClenahan, "The Communality: The Urban Substitute for the Traditional Community," *Sociology and Social Research* 30, no. 4 (1945): 264–74.

4. Seymour B. Sarason, *The Psychological Sense of Community* (San Francisco: Jossey-Bass, 1974).

5. See Richard A. Smith, "Measuring Neighborhood Cohesion: A Review and Some Suggestions," *Human Ecology* 3, no. 3 (1975): 143–60; Thomas Bender, *Community and Social Change in America* (Baltimore: Johns Hopkins University Press, 1982); Robert

N. Bellah et al., *Habits of the Heart: Individualism and Commitment in American Life* (Berkeley: University of California Press, 1985); and David M. Chavis and J. R. Newbrough, "The 'Meaning' of Community in Community Psychology," *Journal of Community Psychology* 14, no. 4 (October 1986): 335–40.

6. David W. McMillan and David M. Chavis, "Sense of Community: A Definition and a Theory," *Journal of Community Psychology* 14 (January 1986): 6–23. In a subsequent paper, written 10 years later, McMillan defines a sense of community as a feeling that members belong together and conform to common norms, rules, and laws so that members know what they can expect from one another; an awareness that members share similar traits so that they can be themselves with one another; and finally, a spirit that comes from shared experiences and is celebrated in traditions. See David W. McMillan, "Sense of Community," *Journal of Community Psychology* 24, no. 4 (1996): 315–25.

7. Albert Hunter, "The Loss of Community: An Empirical Test Through Replication," *American Sociological Review* 40, no. 5 (October 1975): 537–52; Chavis and Newbrough, "The 'Meaning' of Community"; John C. Buckner, "The Development of an Instrument to Measure Neighborhood Cohesion," *American Journal of Community Psychology* 16, no. 6 (1988): 771–91; and William B. Davidson and Patrick R. Cotter, "Sense of Community and Political Participation," *Journal of Community Psychology* 17 (April 1989): 119–25.

8. Davidson and Cotter, "Sense of Community and Political Participation"; Thomas J. Glynn, "Psychological Sense of Community: Measurement and Application," *Human Relations* 34, no. 7 (1981): 789–818; Thomas J. Glynn, "Neighborhood and Sense of Community," *Journal of Community Psychology* 14, no. 4 (October 1986): 341–52; and Sharon Kingston et al., "Sense of Community in Neighborhoods as a Multi-level Construct," *Journal of Community Psychology* 27, no. 6 (1999): 681–94.

9. John D. Kasarda and Morris Janowitz, "Community Attachment in Mass Society," *American Sociological Review* 39, no. 3 (June 1974): 328–39; and Robert J. Sampson, "Linking the Micro- and Macrolevel Dimensions of Community Social Organization," *Social Forces* 70, no. 1 (September 1991): 43–64.

10. Stephanie Riger and Paul J. Lavrakas, "Community Ties: Patterns of Attachment and Social Interaction in Urban Neighborhoods,"

American Journal of Community Psychology 9, no. 1 (1981): 55–66. Studies show people who lead an active family life are more likely to engage in neighborly acts, attend local cultural events, belong to a local organization, know the name of a local leader, and have friends in the neighborhood. Scott Greer, quoted in Wendell Bell, "Social Areas: Typology of Urban Neighborhoods," in *Community Structure and Analysis*, ed. Marvin B. Sussman (New York: Thomas Y. Crowell, 1959): 61–92. People who have friends and relatives in the neighborhood are more likely to feel satisfied with the local community and are less likely to move; those who have relatives living nearby are more likely to have a sense of community, although they are not necessarily more likely to participate in community affairs. See Kasarda and Janowitz, "Community Attachment in Mass Society"; Sampson, "Linking the Micro- and Macrolevel Dimensions"; Jack L. Nasar and David A. Julian, "The Psychological Sense of Community in the Neighborhood," *Journal of the American Planning Association* 61, no. 2 (Spring 1995): 178–84; Jean L. Hill, "Psychological Sense of Community: Suggestions for Future Research," *Journal of Community Psychology* 24, no. 4 (1996): 431–38; Anne S. Brodsky, Patricia J. O'Campo, and Robert E. Aronson, "PSOC in Community Context: Multi-level Correlates of a Measure of Psychological Sense of Community in Low-income, Urban Neighborhoods," *Journal of Community Psychology* 27, no. 6 (1999): 659–79; and John W. Lounsbury, James M. Loveland, and Lucy W. Gibson, "An Investigation of Psychological Sense of Community in Relation to Big Five Personality Traits," *Journal of Community Psychology* 31, no. 5 (2003): 531–41.

11. Riger and Lavrakas, "Community Ties."
12. Karen E. Campbell and Barrett A. Lee, "Sources of Personal Neighbor Networks: Social Integration, Need, or Time?" *Social Forces* 70, no. 4 (June 1992): 1077–1100.
13. Some say that neighborhood-based associations are too small to be called communities, for example: Max Weber, 1947: 136, quoted in Bender, *Community and Social Change*; Davis, *Human Society*; Harold F. Kaufman, "Toward an Interactional Conception of Community," *Social Forces* 38, no. 1 (October 1959): 8–17; Warren, *Community in America*; Sarason, *Psychological Sense of Community*; and Harvey M. Choldin, "Subcommunities: Neighborhoods and Suburbs in Ecological Perspective," in *Sociological Human Ecology: Contemporary Issues and Applications*, ed. Michael

Micklin and Harvey M. Choldin (Boulder, Colo.: Westview Press, 1984), 237–76. Instead of communities, they call them communal relationships (Weber, 1947, quoted in Bender, *Community and Social Change*); sub-communities (Choldin, "Subcommunities: Neighborhoods and Suburbs"); micro-communities (National Research Council, *Toward an Understanding of Metropolitan America* [San Francisco: Canfield Press, 1975], 67); locality groups (George A. Hillery, Jr., "Definitions of Community: Areas of Agreement," *Rural Sociology* 20, no. 2 [June 1955]: 111–23); residential clusters (Michael J. Weiss, *The Clustering of America* [New York: Harper and Row, 1988]); and lifestyle enclaves (Bellah et al., *Habits of the Heart*). Other researchers say that neighborly interactions occur at a smaller scale than that of the neighborhood, and suggest enclaves or groupings of three to 12 dwelling units around a small open space or cul-de-sac. See Nicholas N. Patricios, "The Neighborhood Concept: A Retrospective of Physical Design and Social Interaction," *Journal of Architectural and Planning Research* 19, no. 1 (Spring 2002): 70–90.

14. See Robert E. Park, "The Urban Community as a Spatial Pattern and a Moral Order," in *The Urban Community: Selected Papers from the Proceedings of the American Sociological Society, 1925* (Chicago: University of Chicago Press, 1926), 3–18; Harvey W. Zorbaugh, "The Natural Areas of the City," ibid., 219–29; and Ernest W. Burgess, *Urban Areas of Chicago: An Experiment in Social Science Research* (Chicago: University of Chicago Press, 1929).

> Marcus Vitruvius Pollio believes that community began with the discovery of fire. When people gathered around the fire, sharing its warmth, they began to talk, and this was the beginning of deliberate assembly and social intercourse.

Quoted in R. D. Dripps, *The First House* (Cambridge, Mass.: MIT Press, 1997): 4–5.

15. See Constance Perin, *Everything in Its Place: Social Order and Land Use in America* (Princeton, N.J.: Princeton University Press, 1977); Ray Oldenburg, *The Great Good Place: Cafes, Coffee Shops, Community Centers, Beauty Parlors, General Stores, Bars, Hangouts, and How They Get You Through the Day* (New York: Paragon House, 1989); Eduardo E. Lozano, *Community Design and the Culture of Cities: The Crossroad and the Wall* (New York: Cambridge University

Press, 1990); Sim van der Ryn and Peter Calthorpe, *Sustainable Communities: A New Design Synthesis for Cities, Suburbs and Towns* (San Francisco: Sierra Club, 1991); Andrés Duany and Elizabeth Plater-Zyberk, "The Second Coming of the American Small Town," *Wilson Quarterly* 16 (Winter 1992): 19–51; Peter Calthorpe, *The Next American Metropolis: Ecology, Community, and the American Dream* (New York: Princeton Architectural Press, 1993); James H. Kunstler, *Geography of Nowhere: The Rise and Decline of America's Man-made Landscape* (New York: Simon and Schuster, 1993); P. Langdon, *A Better Place to Live: Reshaping the American Suburb* (Amherst: University of Massachusetts Press, 1994); Peter Katz, *The New Urbanism: Toward an Architecture of Community* (New York: McGraw-Hill, 1994); Gerald A. Porterfield and Kenneth B. Hall, Jr., *A Concise Guide to Community Planning* (New York: McGraw-Hill, 1995), 9; Carter L. Hudgins and Elizabeth Collins Cromley, *Shaping Communities: Perspectives in Vernacular Architecture*, vol. 6 (Knoxville: University of Tennessee Press, 1997); Richard Moe and Carter Wilkie, *Changing Places: Rebuilding Community in the Age of Sprawl* (New York: Henry Holt, 1997); Warren Boeschenstein, *Historic American Towns along the Atlantic Coast* (Baltimore: Johns Hopkins University Press, in association with the Center for American Places, 1999); and U.S. Department of Housing and Urban Development, *State of the Cities Report, 1999* (Washington, D.C.: Department of Housing and Community Development, 1999).

16. See Rene Dubos, "The Biological Basis of Urban Design," in *Anthropopolis: City for Human Development*, ed. C. A. Doxiades (New York: W. W. Norton, 1974), 253–63; and Kirkpatrick Sale, *Human Scale* (London: Secker and Warburg, 1980), 179–81.

17. See Mortimer J. Adler, *Aristotle for Everybody: Difficult Thought Made Easy* (New York: Macmillan, 1978); and Philip Bess, "Design and Happiness: Some Things We Know, Some Things We Have Forgotten" (paper presented at "The New Urbanism: Is Design a Catalyst for Community?" seminar, Seaside, Fla., January 2000).

18. See Dubos, "Biological Basis of Urban Design"; Judith Tannenbaum, "The Neighborhood: A Socio-psychological Analysis," *Land Economics* 24 (February–November 1948): 358–69; Sarason, *Psychological Sense of Community*; Riger and Lavrakas, "Community Ties"; Glynn, "Psychological Sense of Community"; McLaughlin and Davidson, *Builders of the Dawn*; Chavis and

Newbrough, "Meaning of 'Community'"; and Roy F. Baumeister and Mark R. Leary, "The Need to Belong: Desire for Interpersonal Attachments as a Fundamental Human Motivation," *Psychological Bulletin* 117, no. 3 (May 1995): 497–529.

19. See Robert A. Nisbet, *The Quest for Community* (New York: Oxford University Press, 1953).

20. See Richard W. Poston, *Action Now! A Citizen's Guide to Better Communities* (Carbondale: Southern Illinois University Press, 1976); Adam B. Seligman, *The Idea of Civil Society* (New York: Free Press, 1992); Robert D. Putnam, "Tuning In, Tuning Out: The Strange Disappearance of Social Capital in America," *PS: Political Science and Politics*, December 1995, 664–83; and Peter L. Berger and Richard John Neuhaus, *To Empower People: The Role of Mediating Structures in Public Policy* (Washington, D.C.: American Enterprise Institute for Public Policy Research, 1977).

21. Not everyone agrees with this thesis. Some say that what we are seeing is not a loss of community but rather a shift from local communities to citywide or national ones. See the "Controversy Section," *The American Prospect* 25 (March–April 1996): 17–28. It includes essays by Michael Schudson, "What If Civic Life Didn't Die?"; Theda Skocpol, "Unravelling From Above"; Richard M. Valelly, "Couch-potato Democracy?"; and a response by Robert Putnam. See also Barry Wellman, "The Network Community: An Introduction," in *Networks in the Global Village: Life in Contemporary Communities*, ed. Barry Wellman (Boulder, Colo.: Westview Press, 1999), 1–47.

22. Bellah et al., *Habits of the Heart*.

23. See Nisbet, *Quest for Community*, and Poston, *Action Now!*

24. See Putnam, "Tuning In, Tuning Out." However, Wellman argues that the Internet and other digital media have not weakened communities so much as changed them. For example, mobile phones have made possible a form of community that is associated with the individual rather than the household and that links people-wherever-they-are rather than people-in-places. See Barry Wellman, "Physical Place and Cyberspace: The Rise of Personalized Networking," *International Journal of Urban and Regional Research* 25, no. 2 (June 2001): 227–52.

25. See Robert J. Sampson, "Local Friendship Ties and Community Attachment in Mass Society: A Multilevel Systemic Model," *American Sociological Review* 53 (1988): 766–79; McKenzie,

Privatopia; Blakely and Snyder, *Fortress America*; Georjeanna Wilson-Doenges, "An Exploration of Sense of Community and Fear of Crime in Gated Communities," *Environment and Behavior* 32, no. 5 (September 2000): 597–611.

26. See M. P. Baumgartner, *The Moral Order of a Suburb* (New York: Oxford University Press, 1988); Sampson, "Local Friendship Ties"; Claude S. Fischer, "Ambivalent Communities: How Americans Understand Their Localities," in *America at Century's End*, ed. Alan Wolfe (Berkeley: University of California Press, 1991), 79–90; and Lance Freeman, "The Effects of Sprawl on Neighborhood Social Ties: An Explanatory Analysis," *Journal of the American Planning Association* 67, no. 1 (Winter 2001): 69–77.

27. See Hunter, "Loss of Community," 537–52; Richard P. Taub et al., "Urban Voluntary Associations, Locality Based and Externally Induced," *American Journal of Sociology* 83, no. 2 (1977): 425–42; Sale, *Human Scale*; Amos Rapoport, "Neighborhood Heterogeneity or Homogeneity: The Field of Man-Environment Studies," *Architecture and Behavior* 1, no. 1 (1980/81): 65–77; McMillan and Chavis, "Sense of Community"; Steven Edward Cochrun, "Understanding and Enhancing Neighborhood Sense of Community," *Journal of Planning Literature* 9, no. 1 (August 1994): 92–99; Emily Talen, "Sense of Community and Neighborhood Form: An Assessment of the Social Doctrine of New Urbanism," *Urban Studies* 36, no. 8 (1999): 1361–79; and Barry Wellman and Stephanie Potter, "The Elements of Personal Communities," in *Networks in the Global Village: Life in Contemporary Communities*, ed. Barry Wellman (Boulder, Colo.: Westview Press, 1999): 49–81.

28. If a local community's boundaries are no longer set by the neighborhood, how do we know what these boundaries are? Scholars use social network analysis, where they map the flow of messages emanating from individual residents and determine how many of these networks intersect, where they intersect, and whether they intersect at points of local concern. In this way, they can learn the nature and extent of the communities that neighborhood residents belong to and how many of these lie within the physical boundaries of the neighborhood. See Edward O. Laumann, *Bonds of Pluralism: The Form and Substance of Urban Social Networks* (New York: John Wiley and Sons, 1973); Boissevain, *Friends of Friends*; Barry Wellman and Barry Leighton, "Networks, Neighborhoods, and Communities:

Approaches to the Study of the Community Question," *Urban Affairs Quarterly* 14, no. 3 (March 1979): 363–90; Lambert Maguire, *Understanding Social Networks* (Beverly Hills, Calif.: Sage, 1983); Wellman, "The Network Community"; and Wellman and Potter, "Elements of Personal Communities."

29. Interview with A. S., president of the Southwest Community Council (1995), conducted as part of a study by Ralph B. Taylor and Sidney Brower, coprincipal investigators, and Steven Pardue, project director, "Longitudinal Effects of Crime and Signs of Disorder on Communities" (report submitted to the National Institute of Justice, Washington, D.C., 1995). This and the excerpts that follow are taken from interview narratives compiled for the study.

30. Interview conducted in 1997 by Erica Todd, a student in the Urban Studies and Planning Program at the University of Maryland, with leaders of neighborhood-based organizations represented on the Board of the Washington Village/Pigtown Planning Council, in Baltimore.

31. Interview narrative of L. J., past board member of the Canton-Highlandtown Community Association (1994), for Taylor and Brower, "Longitudinal Effects of Crime."

32. Interview narrative of J. C., representative of the Roundhouse Neighborhood Coalition to the Revitalizing Poppleton group (1995), ibid.

33. Interview with M. W., president of the Darley Park Community Association (1995), ibid.

34. Interview with R. T., resident of Columbia, Maryland, 2001.

35. See Hunter, "Loss of Community"; Taub et al., "Urban Voluntary Associations"; Sale, *Human Scale*; Rapoport, "Neighborhood Heterogeneity or Homogeneity"; McMillan and Chavis, "Sense of Community"; Cochrun, "Understanding and Enhancing"; Talen, "Sense of Community"; and Wellman, "The Network Community."

36. See Jean Hill's comment that "once established, psychological sense of community can probably exist, at least for a time, even without interactions, just like any other attachment relationship." Hill, "Psychological Sense of Community."

37. People who are well educated, have a high income, live in a comfortable home, have lived in the neighborhood for a relatively long time, and are above average in church attendance and other kinds of social participation are more likely to engage in neighboring. Caplow, Stryker, and Wallace believe that income is the

essential ingredient for good neighboring, and that increased neighborliness cannot be achieved through social planning but will follow of itself if the general level of welfare is raised. Caplow, Stryker, and Wallace, *Urban Ambience*. Socially prominent people are more likely to think of their local area as a "little community," are more committed to remaining in the neighborhood, and are more likely to take an interest in local community affairs. Kasarda and Janowitz, "Community Attachment in Mass society." Men in high-status groups are more likely to participate in formal organizations and have more social contact with their neighbors, kin, and friends. Bell, "Social Areas." See also Campbell and Lee, "Sources of Personal Neighbor Networks."

38. Weiss, *Clustering of America*; Rapoport, "Neighborhood Heterogeneity or Homogeneity"; and H. Warren Dunham, "The Community Today: Place or Process," *Journal of Community Psychology* 14, no. 4 (October 1986): 402. A longtime resident of Bedford, New York, commenting on the town's tree-preservation ordinance, said: "When I first came to Bedford we didn't need all this legislation, because Bedford was more homogeneous and people could agree on what the place should look like. Now with all these newcomers and development you have to legislate everything because people don't share our taste." In James S. Duncan and Nancy G. Duncan, *Landscapes of Privilege: The Politics of the Aesthetic in an American Suburb* (New York: Routledge, in association with the Center for American Places, 2004), 106.

39. Bell, "Social Areas"; Herbert J. Gans, "Planning and Social Life: Friendship and Neighbor Relations in Suburban Communities," *Journal of the American Institute of Planners* 27, no. 2 (May 1961): 134–40; Herbert J. Gans, "The Balanced Community: Homogeneity or Heterogeneity in Residential areas?" *Journal of the American Institute of Planners* 27, no. 3 (August 1961): 176–84; Gerald D. Suttles, *The Social Construction of Communities* (Chicago: University of Chicago Press, 1972); Rapoport, "Neighborhood Heterogeneity or Homogeneity"; Riger and Lavrakas, "Community Ties"; McLaughlin and Davidson, *Builders of the Dawn*; Weiss, *Clustering of America*; and Fischer, "Ambivalent Communities."

40. See Bellah et al., *Habits of the Heart*; Reginald R. Isaacs, "Attack on the Neighborhood Unit Formula," in *Urban Housing*, ed. L. C. Wheaton, Grace Milgram, and Margie Ellin Meyerson (New York: Free Press, 1966), 94–109; Keyes, *We, The Lonely*

People; and Richard Sennett, *The Fall of Public Man* (London: Faber and Faber, 1986). Blechman raises questions about the social value of age-restricted developments, because while they foster a sense of community among residents, they diminish feelings of responsibility for the larger society. See Andrew D. Blechman, *Leisureville: Adventures in America's Retirement Utopias* (New York: Atlantic Monthly Press, 2008).

41. Interview with K. M., 2001.

42. Ira Iscoe, "Community Psychology and the Competent Community," *American Psychologist* 29, no. 8 (August 1974): 607–13; and Leonard S. Cottrell, Jr., "The Competent Community," in *Further Explorations in Social Psychiatry*, ed. Berton H. Kaplan, Robert N. Wilson, and Alexander H. Leighton (New York: Basic Books, 1976), 195–209.

43. Sutton and Kolaja, "Elements of Community Action"; Robert Booth Fowler, *The Dance with Community: The Contemporary Debate in American Political Thought* (Lawrence: University Press of Kansas, 1991); Leonard A. Jason, *Community Building: Values for a Sustainable Future* (Westport, Conn.: Praeger, 1997); and Joseph Hughey, Paul W. Speer, and N. Andrew Peterson, "Sense of Community in Community Organizations: Structure and Evidence of Validity," *Journal of Community Psychology* 27 (1999): 97–113.

44. Charles P. Loomis, *Social Systems: Essays on Their Persistence and Change* (Princeton, N.J.: Van Nostrand, 1960); Warren, *Community in America*; Suttles, *Social Construction of Communities*; McMillan and Chavis, "Sense of Community"; Michael Neuman, "Utopia, Dystopia, Diaspora," *Journal of the American Planning Association* 57, no. 3 (Summer 1991): 344–47; and Terence R. Lee, "Psychology and Architectural Determinism (Part 2)," *The Architects Journal Information Library*, September 1971, 475–83.

45. Morris Janowitz and Gerald D. Suttles, "The Social Ecology of Citizenship," in *The Management of Human Services*, ed. Rosemary C. Sarri and Yeheskel Hasenfeld (New York: Columbia University Press, 1978), 80–104; and Zane L. Miller, "Self-fulfillment and Decline of Civic Territorial Community," *Journal of Community Psychology* 14, no. 4 (October 1986): 353–64. Janowitz, Suttles, and Miller all define a local community as a group of people who use the same facilities or are in the same service delivery area. Dependence on shared facilities leads to a common interest in their adequacy and the quality of their services. Smith considers

residents' use of local facilities and services a measure of social cohesion. See Smith, "Measuring Neighborhood Cohesion."

46. Scott L. Feld, "The Focused Organization of Social Ties," *American Journal of Sociology* 86, no. 5 (1981): 1015–35.

47. Sherry Boland Ahrentzen, "Managing Conflict by Managing Boundaries: How Professional Homeworkers Cope with Multiple Roles at Home," *Environment and Behavior* 22, no. 6 (November 1990): 723–52.

48. Jan Gehl, *Life Between Buildings: Using Public Space* (New York: Van Nostrand Reinhold, 1987).

49. See, for example, ibid.; and the Baltimore City Department of Planning, *A Year of Celebration* (Washington, D.C.: National Endowment for the Arts, 1977).

50. Sidney Brower, *Good Neighborhoods: A Study of In-Town and Suburban Residential Environments* (Westport, Conn.: Praeger, 1996).

51. See Maruja Torres-Antonini, Mary Joyce Hasell, and John Scanzoni, "Cohousing as a Basis for Social Connectedness and Ecological Sustainability," in *Places, People and Sustainability*, ed. G. Moser et al. (Göttingen, Germany: Hogrefe & Huber, 2002), 125–32; and Tawfiq M. Abu-Ghazzeh, "Housing Layout, Social Interaction, and the Place of Contact in Abu-Nuseir, Jordan," *Journal of Environmental Psychology* 19 (1999): 41–73.

52. Barbara B. Brown and Carol M. Werner, "Social Cohesiveness, Territoriality, and Holiday Decorations: The Influence of Cul-de-sacs," *Environment and Behavior* 17, no. 5 (1985): 539–65; and Donald M. Appleyard, Sue Gerson, and Mark Lintell, *Livable Streets* (Berkeley: University of California Press, 1981).

53. Constance Perin, *Everything in Its Place.*

54. Anthony F. C. Wallace, *Housing and Social Structure: A Preliminary Survey with Particular Reference to Multi-Story, Low-Rent Public Housing Projects* (Philadelphia: Philadelphia Housing Authority, 1952), 41.

55. Chris Webster, "The Nature of the Neighbourhood," *Urban Studies* 40, no. 13 (2003): 2591–612.

56. Duncan and Duncan, *Landscapes of Privilege*, 89.

57. See also Morris Janowitz, *The Community Press in an Urban Setting: The Social Elements of Urbanism* (Chicago: University of Chicago, 1967), 210–13.

58. Gordon Rattray Taylor, *Rethink: A Paraprimitive Solution*; Dolores Hayden, *Seven American Utopias: The Architecture of Communitarian*

Socialism, 1790–1975 (Cambridge, Mass.: MIT Press, 1976); Leopold Kohr, *The Overdeveloped Nations: The Diseconomies of Scale* (Swansea, U.K.: Christopher Davies, 1976); Charles J. Erasmus, *In Search of the Common Good: Utopian Experiments Past and Future* (New York: Free Press, 1977); and Sale, *Human Scale.*

59. Kohr, *Overdeveloped Nations,* 14; and Erasmus, *In Search of the Common Good,* 21.

60. Taylor, *Rethink: A Paraprimitive Solution,* 110; Blumenfeld, Lee, and Doxiades are quoted in Sale, *Human Scale.*

61. Sizes of Utopian communities are from Erasmus, *In Search of the Common Good,* 173; and from Hayden, *Seven American Utopias.* It is worth noting that religious communities have created settings that reflect their particular sets of values. The Mormons, for example, oriented their streets toward the cardinal points; the Shakers insisted on right-angle intersections and symmetrical designs; the Amana community created self-sufficient villages; and the Fourierists and Oneida residents lived in communal buildings. In each of these cases, the community came first, and the community then generated a physical setting. In this book I am suggesting we consider reversing the order: designing a setting so that it will generate a community.

62. Sale, *Human Scale,* 185. The Baltimore neighborhood survey was conducted for the study by Taylor and Brower, "Longitudinal Effects of Crime."

63. Maurice Halbwachs, *The Collective Memory* (New York: Harper and Row, 1980); Bellah et al., *Habits of the Heart,* 154; David Lowenthal, *The Past Is a Foreign Country* (Cambridge, U.K.: Cambridge University Press, 1985), 206, 210; Umberto Eco, "Travels in Hyperreality," in *Travels in Hyperreality: Essays,* trans. William Weaver (New York: Harcourt Brace Jovanovich, 1986), 3–58; Edward S. Casey, *Remembering: A Phenomenological Study* (Bloomington: Indiana University Press, 1987); Michael Kammen, *Mystic Chords of Memory: The Transformation of Tradition in American Culture* (New York: Knopf, 1991); James Fentress and Chris Wickham, *Social Memory* (Cambridge, Mass.: Blackwell, 1992); John Bodnar, *Remaking America: Public Memory, Commemoration, and Patriotism in the Twentieth Century* (Princeton, N.J.: Princeton University Press, 1992); Iwona Inwin-Zarecka, *Frames of Reference: The Dynamics of Collective Memory* (New Brunswick, N.J.: Transaction Press, 1994); and Randall F. Mason, "Memory Infrastructure:

Preservation, 'Improvement,' and Landscapes in New York City, 1898–1925" (PhD dissertation, Columbia University, 1999).

64. Eric Hobsbawm, "Introduction: Inventing Traditions," in *The Invention of Tradition*, ed. Eric Hobsbawm and Terence Ranger (Cambridge, U.K.: Cambridge University Press, 1983); Sandra J. Ball-Rokeach, Yong-Chan Kim, and Sorin Matei, "Storytelling Neighborhood: Paths to Belonging in Diverse Urban Environments," *Communication Research* 28, no. 4 (2001): 392–428; and David Glassberg, *American Historical Pageantry: The Uses of Tradition in the Early Twentieth Century* (Chapel Hill: University of North Carolina Press, 1990).

65. S. Torri, unpublished doctoral dissertation (University 'La Sapienza,' Rome, Italy), reported in Miretta Prezza, Matilde Arnici, Tiziana Roberti, and Gloria Tedeschi, "Sense of Community Referred to the Whole Town: Its Relations with Neighboring, Loneliness, Life Satisfaction, and Area of Residence," *Journal of Community Psychology* 29, no. 1 (2001): 29–52.

66. Buckner, in "Development of an Instrument," refers to these as "cohesive settings."

67. Howard Gillette Jr. takes a similar approach in his book *Civitas by Design: Building Better Communities from the Garden City to the New Urbanism* (Philadelphia: University of Pennsylvania, 2010).

68. I realize that my choices do not represent the full range of residential settings, but I feel that they are reasonably representative of community designs in the United States.

69. I have chosen not to present the communities in the form of case studies, which require full-blown descriptions and across-case comparisons that do not further my line of enquiry.

CHAPTER 2

1. Walden Fawcett, "Roland Park, Baltimore County, Maryland: A Representative American Suburb," *House and Garden* 11, no. 4 (April 1903): 195.

2. The description of Roland Park draws on Fawcett, "Roland Park," 175–97; Village of Cross Keys, *Reflections on Roland Park* (Baltimore: Community Research and Development, the Rouse Company, 1963); Harry G. Schalck, "Mini-revisionism in City Planning History: The Planners of Roland Park," *Journal of the*

Society of Architectural Historians 29, no. 4 (December 1970): 347–49; James F. Waesche, *Crowning the Gravelly Hill: A History of the Roland Park–Guilford–Homeland District* (Baltimore: Maclay & Associates, 1987); Roberta M. Moudry, "Frederick Law Olmsted, Sr.'s Roland Park: The Idea of a Suburb" (paper presented to the Friends of Maryland's Olmsted Parks and Landscapes, Baltimore, May 22, 1990); and from the author's personal observations.

3. Fawcett, "Roland Park," 185.

4. The *Roland Park Review* was first published in March 1907. Waesche, *Crowning the Gravelly Hill*, 72.

5. Ibid., 55.

6. Ibid., 71.

7. Schalck, "Mini-revisionism in City Planning History," 424.

8. The description of Radburn draws heavily on Robert B. Hudson, *Radburn: A Plan for Living* (New York: American Association for Adult Education, 1934); Clarence S. Stein, *Toward New Towns for America* (Cambridge, Mass.: MIT Press, 1966); Eugenie Ladner Birch, "Radburn and the American Planning Movement: The Persistence of an Idea," *Journal of the American Planning Association* 46, no. 4 (October 1980): 424–39; Daniel Schaffer, *Garden Cities for America: The Radburn Experience* (Philadelphia: Temple University Press, 1982); and Chang-Moo Lee and Kun-Hyuck Ahn, "Is Kentlands Better Than Radburn? The American Garden City and New Urbanist Paradigms," *Journal of the American Planning Association* 69, no. 1 (Winter 2003): 50–71.

9. Actually, Mariemont, Ohio (1922), was the first completed example of garden city planning in the United States. See chapter 5 for a description of Mariemont.

10. Declaration of Restrictions No. 1 Affecting Radburn, Property of City Housing Corporation in the Borough of Fair Lawn, Bergen County, N.J. (March 16, 1929).

11. In practice, the front doors are little used, and most pedestrian life, including children's play, occurs on the "service" roads. See Hans Blumenfeld, *Metropolis . . . And Beyond: Selected Essays*, ed. Paul D. Spreiregan (New York: John Wiley, 1979), 149.

12. Schaffer, *Garden Cities for America*, 162.

13. Ibid., 177.

14. Schaffer notes that the first residents were attracted to Radburn more by its pleasant environment and well-equipped homes than by any desire to move into an experimental community.

15. These included the Radburn Players, the Radburn Singers, Friends of Music, a garden club, and various discussion groups concerned with, among other topics, music appreciation, international affairs, contemporary literature, nutrition, public speaking, and arts and crafts.

16. Hudson, *Radburn: A Plan for Living*, 88, 3.

17. Information about the Twin Oaks Community comes from Kathleen Kinkade, *A Walden Two Experiment: The First Five Years of Twin Oaks Community* (New York: Quill, 1973); Kathleen Kinkade, *Is It Utopia Yet? An Insider's View of Twin Oaks Community in Its 26th Year* (Twin Oaks Community, Va.: Twin Oaks Publishing, 1994); I. Komar, *Living the Dream: A Documentary Study of the Twin Oaks Community* (Norwood, Pa.: Norwood Editions, 1983); the Twin Oaks Community website, http://twinoaks.org; and comments made by the resident guide when I visited Twin Oaks in 2002.

18. B. F. Skinner, *Walden Two* (New York: Macmillan, 1976).

19. McLaughlin and Davidson write that "an intentional community, as distinct from a neighborhood or town, is a group of people experiencing a common purpose in being together." McLaughlin and Davidson, *Builders of the Dawn.* See also Barry Shenker, *Intentional Communities: Ideologies and Alienation in Communal Societies* (Boston: Routledge & Kegan Paul, 1986); and the Intentional Communities website, www.ic.org.

20. Information about Seaside comes mainly from Steven Brooke, *Seaside* (Gretna, La.: Pelican, 1995); and David Mohney and Keller Easterling, eds., *Seaside: Making a Town in America* (New York: Princeton Architectural Press, 1991).

21. For more about his ideas, see Léon Krier, *The Architecture of Community* (Washington, D.C.: Island Press, 2009).

22. One accommodation night equals one night rental irrespective of the size of the cottage. Numbers are from the Seaside Institute Special Projects Manager via e-mail, August 12, 2010.

23. New urbanism is an urban design movement that emerged in the United States in the early 1980s and promotes walkable neighborhoods. The movement endorses the features listed here. The organizing body for new urbanism is the Congress for the New Urbanism, founded in 1993.

24. Andrés Duany and Elizabeth Plater-Zyberk, "The Second Coming of the American Small Town," *Wilson Quarterly* 16 (Winter 1992): 19–51; and Bressi, "Planning the American Dream."

25. Katz, *The New Urbanism*, 3.

26. *Seaside Times*, Summer 1999.

27. Andrés Duany, Elizabeth Plater-Zyberk, and Jeff Speck, *Suburban Nation: The Rise of Sprawl and the Decline of the American Dream* (New York: North Point Press, 2000), 209.

28. Jeanne M. Plas and Susan E. Lewis, "Environmental Factors and Sense of Community in a Planned Town," *American Journal of Community Psychology* 24, no. 1 (1996): 109–43.

CHAPTER 3

1. Georges Simenon, *Maigret and the Toy Village*, trans. Eileen Ellenbogen (New York: Harcourt Brace Jovanovich, 1979), 82.

2. Information about Carmel-by-the-Sea is drawn from Harold Gilliam and Ann Gilliam, *Creating Carmel: The Enduring Vision* (Layton, Utah: Gibbs Smith, 1992); several documents from the City of Carmel-by-the-Sea, including *The Housing Element* (December 6, 1994); *Draft Historic Preservation Element* (October 3, 2000; revised February 9, 2001); and Ordinance No. 2001-09: An Ordinance Amending the City's Design Standards and Review Processes for Properties in All Commercial and R-4 Districts (2001); and from the author's personal observations, 2002.

3. Quoted in Gilliam and Gilliam, *Creating Carmel*, 77.

4. Ibid., 69.

5. *Los Angeles Times*, May 22, 1910, quoted ibid., 85.

6. Quoted in Gilliam and Gilliam, *Creating Carmel*, 177.

7. Patricia Leigh Brown, "Fighting for a Carrier-free Zone: Carmel Debates the Merits of Mail Delivery," *New York Times*, September 6, 2000, A14.

8. City of Carmel-by-the-Sea, *Housing Element*, 3–31.

9. For information about Levittown, I have drawn on John Thomas Liell, "Levittown: A Study in Community Planning and Development" (Ph.D. dissertation, Yale University, 1952); William J. Levitt, "A House Is Not Enough: The Story of America's First Community Builder," in *Business Decisions That Changed Our Lives*, ed. Sidney Furst and Milton Sherman (New York: Random House, 1964), 59–71; and Barbara M. Kelly, *Expanding the American Dream: Building and Rebuilding Levittown* (Albany: State University of New York Press, 1993).

10. Abraham Levitt said at this time, "Our purpose is to make [Levittown] a complete integrated harmonious community. We aim, among other things, to provide a pleasant and wholesome social life." Quoted in Liell, "Levittown: A Study," 117. The swimming pools were later handed over to the town, which set up a special tax district in order to operate them. Residents complained that the stores in the greens were overcharging and that service was perfunctory and impolite, and many of them took their business out of Levittown to the surrounding areas.

11. Liell, "Levittown: A Study," 171.

12. These restrictions were officially removed after the 1948 U.S. Supreme Court decision in *Shelley v. Kraemer* made racial discrimination unconstitutional.

13. Rosalyn Baxandall and Elizabeth Ewen, *Picture Windows: How the Suburbs Happened* (New York: Basic Books, 2000), 156.

14. Geoffrey Mohan, "Levittown at Fifty: Suburban Pioneers," available at http.uta.fi/FAST/US2/REF/levit-50.html.

15. Corey Kilgannon, "As Levittown Houses Change, Memories from a Famous Suburb Fade," *New York Times*, October 13, 2007, B10.

16. Herbert J. Gans, *The Levittowners: Ways of Life and Politics in a New Suburban Community* (New York: Random House, 1967).

17. Taylor and Brower, "Longitudinal Effects of Crime."

18. The description of Celebration draws heavily on The Celebration Company, *Downtown Celebration: Architectural Walking Tour* (Celebration, Fla.: The Celebration Company, 1996); Douglas Frantz and Catherine Collins, *Celebration U.S.A.: Living in Disney's Brave New World* (New York: Henry Holt, 1999); Andrew Ross, *The Celebration Chronicles: Life, Liberty, and the Pursuit of Property Values in Disney's New Town* (New York: Ballantine, 1999); and Michael Lassell, *Celebration: The Story of a Town* (New York: Disney Enterprises, 2004).

19. Russ Rymer, "Back to the Future: Disney Reinvents the Company Town," *Harper's Magazine* 293, no. 1757 (October 1996): 65–76.

20. Ross, *Celebration Chronicles*, 84.

21. Frantz and Collins, *Celebration U.S.A.*, 247.

22. Ross, *Celebration Chronicles*, 88.

23. Frantz and Collins, *Celebration U.S.A.*, 154.

24. Ross, *Celebration Chronicles*, 213. Because Celebration is, in effect, a company town, The Celebration Company also fosters community in an altogether unintended way: It represents a single target

for complaints, something against which residents can rally when anything goes wrong. This was demonstrated quite early, when a group of parents got together to object to the quality of education in the school. See Michael Pollan, "Disney Discovers Real Life," *New York Times Magazine*, December 14, 1997, 56–88.

25. See www.celebration.fl.us.
26. Ross, *Celebration Chronicles*, 207.
27. Frantz and Collins, *Celebration U.S.A.*, 84.
28. Ross, *Celebration Chronicles*, 215.
29. Abby Goodnough, "Disney Is Selling a Town It Built to Reflect the Past," *New York Times*, January 16, 2004, A10.
30. The Celebration Company, *Downtown Celebration*, 7.
31. Information about this community comes mainly from interviews conducted in the fall of 2001 by me and graduate students in my class URSP 688C at the University of Maryland. We interviewed six directors of the home owners association and a representative of the management company. The president of the home owners association was unhappy with the interview findings and asked that I not use the community's true name.
32. Vicky Carlstrand, "How to Behave in the Garden," *Financial Times*, February 5, 2000, 21
33. "Metropolitan Diary," *New York Times*, June 5, 2000, A28.

CHAPTER 4

1. Raymond Unwin, chapter 1 of *Town Planning in Practice: An Intro-duction to the Art of Designing Cities and Suburbs* [1909], in *The Legacy of Raymond Unwin: A Human Pattern for Planning*, Walter L. Creese (Cambridge, Mass.: MIT Press, 1967), 106.
2. Stein, *Toward New Towns*, 60.
3. Frederick Law Olmsted, "Preliminary Report upon the Proposed Suburban Village at Riverside, near Chicago [1868]," in *The Years of Olmsted, Vaux and Company, 1865–1874*, ed. David Schuyler and Jane Turner Censer (Baltimore: Johns Hopkins University Press, 1992), 6: 273–90. Information about Riverside comes mainly from Olmstead, "Preliminary Report"; Riverside Improvement Company, *Riverside in 1871, with a Description of Its Improvements Together with Some Engravings of Views and Buildings* (1871; repr., Riverside, Ill.: Riverside Historical Commission, n.d.); Laura

Wood Roper, *FLO: A Biography of Frederick Law Olmsted* (Baltimore: Johns Hopkins University Press, 1973); David Schuyler, "Frederick Law Olmsted's Riverside," *Planning History Present 7*, no. 2 (1993); Charles E. Beveridge and Paul Rocheleau, *Frederick Law Olmsted: Designing the American Landscape* (New York: Rizzoli, 1995), 117–23; Witold Rybczynski, *A Clearing in the Distance: Frederick Law Olmsted and America in the 19th Century* (New York: Simon and Schuster, 1999); and Sarah Faiks, Jarrett Kest, Amanda Szot, and Molly Vendura, "Revisiting Riverside: A Frederick Law Olmsted Community" (master's project, School of Natural Resources and Environment, University of Michigan, 2001).

4. Riverside Improvement Company, *Riverside in 1871*, 9. Olmsted also provided a number of smaller, rail-side lots for the working classes. The Riverside Improvement Company described Riverside as a place for both the merchant and his clerk.

5. Ibid., 13.

6. Riverside community website, http.riverside-illinois.com.

7. Information about garden cities comes from Ebenezer Howard, *Garden Cities of Tomorrow* [1902] (Cambridge, Mass.: MIT Press, 1965). (Originally published in 1898 as *Tomorrow: A Peaceful Path to Real Reform*.) Information about Letchworth comes from Unwin, "Town Planning"; C. B. Purdom, *The Garden City: A Study in the Development of a Modern Town* (1913; repr., New York: Garland, 1985); C. B. Purdom, *The Building of Satellite Towns*, rev. ed. (London: J. M. Dent and Sons, 1949); C. B. Purdom, *The Letchworth Achievement* (London: J. M. Dent and Sons, 1963); Frank Jackson, *Sir Raymond Unwin: Architect, Planner and Visionary* (London: Zwemmer, 1985); Mervyn Miller, *Raymond Unwin: Garden Cities and Town Planning* (London: Leicester University Press, 1992); and the website for Letchworth Garden City, www.letchworthgardencity.net.

8. Jonathan Glancey, "They Don't Make Them Like They Used To," *Guardian*, December 1, 2003. It is interesting to compare the comments that were made about the early residents of Letchworth with those about Carmel-by-the-Sea, discussed in chapter 3. People who feel that they do not fit into the mainstream community find the idea of creating a new (and hopefully more compatible) one especially attractive.

9. W. P. Westell, *The Country Home*, 69 (June 1909), available at www.letchworthgardencity.net/lgcs/westrell.htm.

10. It is interesting to note that Unwin had proposed this form of collective housing in a lecture given some years earlier. The lecture, called "Cooperation in Building," is quoted in Barry Parker, *The Art of Building a Home: A Collection of Lectures and Illustrations by Barry Parker and Raymond Unwin*, 2nd ed. (New York: Longmans, Green and Co., 1901): 91–108. It includes the following:

> Why should not cottages be grouped into quadrangles, having all of the available land in a square in the center? Some of the space so often wasted in a useless front parlour in each cottage, could be used to form instead a Common Room, in which a fire might always be burning in an evening, where comfort for social intercourse, for reading, or writing, could always be found . . . To this Common Room could be added a laundry and drying-room fitted with a few modern appliances which would . . . take the bulky copper and mangle out of each cottage, and relieve them all of the unpleasantness of the steam and encumbrance of the drying clothes. In connection with this a bathroom could be arranged for groups of the smallest cottages, while the growth of co-operation would soon bring the common bakehouse and kitchen. From this to the preparation of meals and the serving of them in the common room would be only a matter of time.

11. Ibid., 92.
12. Information about the neighborhood unit formula comes from Clarence A. Perry, "The Local Community as a Unit in the Planning of Urban Residential Areas," in *The Urban Community: Selected Papers from the Proceedings of the American Sociological Society, 1925*, ed. Ernest W. Burgess (Chicago: University of Chicago Press, 1926): 238–41; Clarence A. Perry, "The Neighborhood Unit," monograph in *Neighborhood and Community Planning*, Regional Survey, vol. 7 (New York: Regional Plan of New York and Its Environs, 1929); Clarence A. Perry, "The Neighborhood Unit Formula" [1939], in *Urban Housing*, ed. L. C. Wheaton, Grace Milgram, and Margie Ellin Meyerson (New York: Free Press, 1966), 94–109; and Clarence A. Perry, *Housing for the Machine Age* (New York: Russell Sage Foundation, 1939).
13. Clarence S. Stein and Catherine Bauer, "Store Buildings and Neighborhood Shopping Centers," *Architectural Record*, February 1934, 175–87.

14. Perry, *Housing for the Machine Age*, 41.

15. Ibid., 215.

16. The United Kingdom's New Towns Act of 1946 (and subsequent acts) led to the designation of 11 new towns between 1946 and 1955. The first group of towns was developed using the principles set out by Ebenezer Howard.

17. J. E. Gibson, *Designing the New City: A Systemic Approach* (New York: Wiley, 1977), 169–70.

18. Information about Columbia comes from the Village of Cross Keys, *Reflections on Roland Park*; The Rouse Company, *Columbia: A New City* (Baltimore: The Rouse Company, 1966); Edward P. Eichler and Marshall Kaplan, *The Community Builders* (Berkeley: University of California Press, 1967); Morton Hoppenfeld, "A Sketch of the Planning-building Process for Columbia, Maryland," *Journal of the American Institute of Planners* 33, no. 5 (November 1967): 398–409; Richard Oliver Brooks, *New Towns and Communal Values: A Case Study of Columbia, Maryland* (New York: Praeger, 1974); James W. Rouse, "Building a Sense of Place," in *Psychology of the Planner Community: The New Town Experience*, ed. Donald C. Klein (New York: Human Sciences Press, 1978), 51–7; Lynn C. Burkhart, *Old Values in a New Town: The Politics of Race and Class in Columbia, Maryland* (New York: Praeger, 1981); Robert Tennenbaum, "Hail, Columbia," *Planning* 56, no. 5 (May 1990): 16–17; and Robert Tennenbaum, ed., *Creating a New City: Columbia, Maryland* (Columbia, Md.: Perry Publishing, 1996); Columbia Association, *CA Guide: Columbia Association's Handbook for Residents, 2000–2001* (Columbia, Md.: Columbia Association, 2000); Angela Paik, "Leader of Columbia Focus of Growing Ire: Her Style, Absences Criticized at Meeting," *Washington Post*, March 20, 2000, B01; and from my conversations with Robert Tennenbaum, Barbara Kellner, and Katherine Mann, the assistant manager for the Village of Long Reach, Columbia, 2001. Unless otherwise noted, the quotations are from interviews with residents of Columbia conducted in 2001 by me and my graduate assistants at the University of Maryland.

19. Robert Nusgart, "Columbia's Final Piece," *Baltimore Sun*, January 18, 1998, 2L.

20. James W. Rouse, quoted in Tennenbaum, *Creating a New City*, ix.

21. Paik, "Leader of Columbia."

22. Burkhart, *Old Values in a New Town*.

23. Mitchell and Stebenne quote a memo from James Rouse in which he stated, "People grow best in small communities of 5,000 to 10,000 people, where the institutions that are the dominant forces in their lives are within the scale of their comprehension and sense of responsibility." Joseph R. Mitchell and David L. Stebenne, *New City upon a Hill: A History of Columbia, Maryland* (Charleston, S.C.: The History Press, 2007), 71.

24. Nusgart, "Columbia's Final Piece." According to Eichler and Kaplan, *The Community Builders*, 67, the work group had proposed that the stores be subsidized, be owned and operated by a communitywide nonprofit organization, and serve as combination restaurant-meeting halls—places to distribute information about community affairs.

25. Laura Vozzella, "Hoping to Alter a Retail Worry," *Baltimore Sun*, May 2001, 1B.

26. Information about Lake Claire Cohousing comes from author's observations and discussions with the architect, Greg Ramsey, at Lake Claire Cohousing, 2000; D. Lindeman, "Southern Comfort: Cohousing on a Small Urban Site. Community Spotlight: Lake Claire Commons, GA," *CoHousing*, article no. 1 (Winter 2000); D. Lindeman, "Designing for Small Spaces: A Tour of Lake Claire Commons," *CoHousing*, article no. 2 (Winter 2000); Maruja Torres-Antonini, "Our Common House: Using the Built Environment to Develop Supportive Communities" (Ph.D. dissertation, University of Florida, 2001); Torres-Antonini, Hasell, and Scanzoni, "Cohousing as a Basis for Social Connectedness"; and the Intentional Communities website, www.fic.ic.org.

27. See Kathryn McCamant and Charles Durrett, *Cohousing: A Contemporary Approach to Housing Ourselves* (Berkeley, Calif.: Habitat Press, 1988); Dorit Fromm, *Collaborative Communities*; William Lennertz, "Town-making Fundamentals," in *Towns and Town-Making Principles*, Andrés Duany and Elizabeth Plater-Zyberk, ed. Alex Krieger (New York: Rizzoli, 1991), 21–24; and Clare Cooper Marcus, "Site Planning, Building Design and a Sense of Community: An Analysis of Six Cohousing Schemes in Denmark, Sweden, and the Netherlands," *Journal of Architectural and Planning Research* 17, no. 2 (Summer 2000): 146–63.

28. Torres-Antonini, "Our Common House"; and Torres-Antonini et al., "Cohousing as a Basis for Social Connectedness."

29. Olmsted, "Preliminary Report," 286.

CHAPTER 5

1. Bellah et al., *Habits of the Heart*, 153.
2. Information about Santa Fe comes mainly from Chris Wilson, *The Myth of Santa Fe: Creating a Modern Regional Tradition* (Albuquerque: University of New Mexico Press, 1997).
3. Quoted in ibid., 237.
4. Quoted in ibid., 130.
5. Quoted in ibid., 254.
6. Quoted in ibid., 256.
7. Information about Chadds Ford comes mainly from John D. Dorst, *The Written Suburb: An American Site, An Ethnographic Dilemma* (Philadelphia: University of Pennsylvania Press, 1989).
8. Scott Saxman, "Chadds Ford: 'A Hidden Suburb'" (student paper, Community Planning Program, University of Maryland, December 2001).
9. Ibid.
10. Information about Mariemont comes mainly from John L. Hancock, "John Nolen and the American City-Planning Movement: A History of Culture Change and Community Response, 1900–1940" (Ph.D. dissertation, University of Pennsylvania, 1964); Kevin B. Sullivan, "Mariemont, Ohio: Three Papers" (papers for GSD 3102, Harvard University, Cambridge, Mass., November 12, 1992); Bradley D. Cross, "Making History: The Search for Civic and Cultural Identity in an American New Town, 1940–1980," in *Making Sense Out of the Urban Environment: Local Government, Civic Culture, and Community Life in American Cities*, ed. Robert Fairbanks and Patricia Melvin-Mooney (Columbus: Ohio State University Press, 2001), 138–55; and Millard F. Rogers, Jr., *John Nolen and Mariemont: Building a New Town in Ohio* (Baltimore: Johns Hopkins University Press, in association with the Center for American Places, 2001).
11. John Nolen, *New Towns for Old: Achievements in Civic Improvement in Some American Small Towns and Neighborhoods* (Boston: Marshall Jones Company, 1927), 126.
12. Information about Opa-locka comes from Frank S. FitzGerald-Bush, *A Dream of Araby: Glenn H. Curtiss and the Founding of Opa-locka* (Opa-locka, Fla.: South Florida Archaeological Museum, 1976); and Catherine Lynn, "Dream and Substance: Araby and the Planning of Opa-locka," *Journal of Decorative and Propaganda Arts* 23 (1998): 162–89.

13. For alternative versions of the origins of the design, see Lynn, "Dream and Substance," 164.

14. In the documentary film *Salesman*, a door-to-door Bible salesman tells how he gets completely lost in "the Moslem district." Albert Maysles, David Maysles, and Charlotte Zwerin, dirs., *Salesman* (Maysles Films, 1968).

15. Michael Brick, "'Rat-filled Beats 'Historic,' So City Offices Move Out," *New York Times*, March 16, 2007, A16.

CHAPTER 6

1. Christopher Alexander, *A New Theory of Urban Design* (New York: Oxford University Press, 1987), 2.

2. Amos Rapoport, *Culture, Architecture, and Design* (Chicago: Locke Science Publishing, 2005), 1.

3. Raymond Unwin, quoted in Mervyn Miller, *Raymond Unwin*, 110.

4. See Lindeman, "Designing for Small Spaces: A Tour of Lake Claire Commons," *Cohousing Magazine*, article no. 2 (Summer 2000), 6.

5. Stein, *Toward New Towns*, 226.

6. Morgan puts it this way:

> The modern town planner, in trying to secure an impression of integration and unity in the physical planning of a village, tries to find an axis or a focus for his plan. Sometimes, without fully realizing the significance of what he does, he tries to secure outward visible evidence of an inward and spiritual condition which would characterize a true community.

Arthur E. Morgan, "Homo Sapiens: The Community Animal," in *The Company of Others: Making Community in the Modern World*, ed. Claude Whitmyer (New York: Jeremy P. Tarcher/Perigee, 1993), 16–19.

7. Henry Moore, *Henry Moore on Sculpture*, ed. Philip James (New York: Viking, 1971), 64.

8. Donald A. Schön, *The Reflective Practitioner* (New York: Basic Books, 1983); and Peter Rowe, *Design Thinking* (Cambridge, Mass.: MIT Press, 1986).

9. Porterfield and Hall, *Concise Guide to Community Planning*, 13

10. Stein, *Toward New Towns*, 225.

11. For more about lifestyle and experience marketing, see Sharon Zukin, *Point of Purchase: How Shopping Changed American Culture* (New York: Routledge, 2004); and B. Joseph Pine II and James H. Gilmore, *The Experience Economy: Work Is Theatre and Every Business Is a Stage* (Boston: Harvard Business Review Press, 1999).

12. Ross, *Celebration Chronicles*, 18.

13. Glynis M. Breakwell, *Coping with Threatened Identities* (London: Methuen, 1986). See also Clare Twigger-Ross and David Uzzell, "Place and Identity Processes," *Journal of Environmental Psychology* 16 (1996): 205–20; and Lynn C. Manzo, "Beyond House and Haven: Toward a Revisioning of Emotional Relationships with Places," *Journal of Environmental Psychology* 23, no. 1 (2003): 47–61.

14. Kammen, *Mystic Chords of Memory*, 676–77; and J. S. Wood and M. Steinitz, "A World We Have Gained: House, Common, and Village in New England," *Journal of Historical Geography* 18, no. 1 (1992): 105–20.

15. Information about Frankenmuth comes from Herman F. Zehnder, *Teach My People the Truth: The Story of Frankenmuth, Michigan* (Frankenmuth, Mich.: H. F. Zehnder, 1969).

16. Susan McKee, "Frankenmuth, Michigan," *German Life*, June/July 1999.

17. Candus Thompson, "In Town, Life Imitates Artwork," *Baltimore Sun*, November 29, 2001, 32A.

18. Lisa Gray, "Home to Mayberry," *Slate* (July 31, 2001), www.slate.com/id/112824.

19. I raised the question of design ethics in chapter 5, when questioning designs that present a false history. I raise it again in chapter 7, when discussing the qualities of a good neighborhood.

20. There is a myth that in 1787, Grigory Potemkin, a minister of Catherine the Great, erected hollow façades of villages along a route the empress was to travel, in order to give her a false impression of the prosperity of the region. *Encyclopaedia Britannica Online*, s.v. "Potemkin, Grigory Aleksandrovich," http.britannica.com/EBchecked/topic/472610/Grigory-Aleksandrovich-Potemkin.

21. James and Nancy Duncan write, "It can be argued . . . that there is an aesthetic of community that celebrates 'sign values' of close neighborly relations that obscures a lack of more fully developed communal relations." Duncan and Duncan, *Landscapes of Privilege*, 26.

CHAPTER 7

1. James Rouse, quoted in Hoppenfeld, "Sketch of the Planning-building Process."
2. Sidney Brower, "Design in Familiar Places" (report to the National Endowment for the Arts, Washington, D.C., 1985).
3. See Dan Houston, Michael Oden, and William Spelman, "Big Box Retail and Austin: An Independent Review" (report prepared for the Austin Independent Business Alliance, Austin Full Circle, Livable City, and AFSCME Local 1624, October 6, 2004), www .civiceconomics.com/big_box_review_final.pdf.
4. Léon Krier, *Architecture of Community*, 135.
5. See Gehl, *Life Between Buildings*; and the Baltimore City Department of Planning, *A Year of Celebration*.
6. Interview with K. M., 2001.
7. John Nolen, *New Towns for Old*, 110.
8. See Caplow, Stryker, and Wallace, *Urban Ambience*. They identify the following network patterns: tribal, intimate, casual, clique, ring-around-the-rosie, and anomie (the latter "not a meaningful social entity"). See also Jeremy Boissevain's classification of coalitions as cliques, gangs, action sets, and factions, in *Friends of Friends*. For a discussion of community typologies, see Christen T. Jonassen, "Community Typology," in *Community Structure and Analysis*, ed. Marvin B. Sussman (New York: Thomas Y. Crowell, 1959), 15–36. My typology has a loose relationship to the four types of neighborhoods seen in Brower, *Good Neighborhoods*.
9. This type fits Tönnies's definition of *Gesellschaft*—a relationship that is transitory and superficial—whereas the tribal type fits his definition of *Gemeinschaft*, "the lasting and genuine form of living together." See Ferdinand Tönnies, "Gemeinschaft and Gesellschaft," in *The Sociology of Community: A Selection of Readings*, ed. Colin Bell and Howard Newby (London: Frank Cass and Co., 1974), 8–12.
10. See Isaacs, "Attack on the Neighborhood Unit"; Keyes, *We, the Lonely People*; and Sennett, *Fall of Public Man*.
11. For a discussion of membership criteria that are considered to be socially acceptable and how these criteria have changed over time, see Janny Scott, "Debating Which Private Clubs Are Acceptable. And Private," *New York Times*, December 5, 2002, Week in Review, 5.

12. Rouse, "It Can Happen Here."
13. Roland L. Warren, "The Good Community Revisited," *Social Development Issues* 4, no. 3 (Fall 1980): 18–40.
14. The neighborhoods and neighborhood centers in Columbia have no administrative function, and they have little social significance for residents.
15. Fried asked 2,622 respondents about their residential experience. When asked about the qualities of an ideal neighborhood, more people (24.4 percent) indicated a preference for privacy and social distance than desired or even indirectly implied wishes for social interaction (21.1 percent). Marc Fried, "Residential Attachment: Sources of Residential and Community Satisfaction," *Journal of Social Issues* 38, no. 3 (1982): 107–19.

CHAPTER 8

1. Duany, Plater-Zyberk, and Speck, *Suburban Nation*, 217.
2. Fowler, *Dance with Community*, 45.
3. Sidney Brower, "The Corner Store as an Element of Smart Growth" (study presented at Smart Growth @10 Conference, College Park, Maryland, October 2007), www.rff.org/rff/events/upload/30226_1.pdf. I gratefully acknowledge help from three University of Maryland students who worked as my research assistants in the study: Rachel Fitzgerald did many of the interviews, compiled responses, and prepared the graphics; and Vikas Mehta and Shannon Grevious unearthed written material about corner stores.
4. See Calthorpe, *Next American Metropolis*; Duany, Plater-Zyberk, and Speck, *Suburban Nation*; Michael D. Beyard, Michael Pawlukiewicz, and Alex Bond, *Ten Principles for Rebuilding Neighborhood Retail* (Washington, D.C.: Urban Land Institute, 2003); Emily Talen, *New Urbanism and American Planning: The Conflict of Cultures* (New York: Routledge, 2005); and the Smart Growth Network and ICMA, "Getting to Smart Growth: 100 Policies for Implementation," www.smartgrowth.org/pdf/gettosg.pdf.
5. Jill Rosen, "Rezoning Reveals Clash of Fells Point Cultures," *Baltimore Sun*, September 11, 2005, 1A, 22A.
6. I noted in the introduction that this urban pattern is found in Locust Point, Baltimore. See City Commission for Historical and

Architectural Preservation, National Register of Historic Places Inventory Nomination Form, Canton Historic District Nomination, Baltimore, 1978; Norman Rukert, *Historic Canton* (Baltimore: Bodine & Associates, 1978); Natalie W. Shivers, *Those Placid Rows* (Baltimore: Maclay and Associates, 1981); and Mary Ellen Hayward and Charles Belfoure, *The Baltimore Rowhouse* (New York: Princeton Architectural Press, 1999).

7. For general information about changes in marketing, see Richard S. Tedlow, *New and Improved: The Story of Mass Marketing in America* (New York: Basic Books, 1990); David Monad, *Store Wars: Shopkeepers and the Culture of Mass Marketing, 1890–1939* (Toronto: University of Toronto Press, 1996); and Zukin, *Point of Purchase.* A 1990 survey showed that people's decisions about where to shop and what to buy are made more on the basis of price than location. Robert A. Peterson, ed., *The Future of U.S. Retailing: An Agenda for the 21st Century* (New York: Quorum Books, 1992), 53. Small stores also have to compete with home shopping, made easier and more convenient by the Internet. The Direct Selling Association reports that in 2008, more than 74 percent of Americans purchased goods or services through direct selling. Direct Selling Association, "FAQs," www.dsa.org/about/faq. See also Dominique Xardel, *The Direct Selling Revolution* (Cambridge, Mass.: Blackwell, 1993); and Ted C. Fishman, "Click Here for Tomatoes," http://money.cnn.com/magazines/moneymag/moneymag_archive/2005/04/01/8254993/index.htm. When residents can shop without having to leave home, the location of the store is irrelevant.

8. A Kash n' Karry store in Fort Myers, Florida, is described as follows:

> The bright, energetic decor; the keen focus on food, and especially fresh food presentation; the proliferation of informative and often playful signage; the butchers, bakers, fishmongers, and other assorted "taste ambassadors" selling entertainment as well as canned peas—the entire package is geared toward generating excitement about buying, cooking and eating food.

Stephen Dowdell, "Passion Play," April 3, 2005, www.allbusiness.com/retail-trade/4265736-1.html. See also Michael Barbaro, "Ideas and Trends: In Aisle Three, Couch Potatoes Trying the MP3s," *New York Times*, March 18, 2007.

9. Rocco Pendola and Sheldon Gen, "Does 'Main Street' Promote Sense of Community? A Comparison of San Francisco Neighborhoods," *Environment and Behavior* 40, no. 4 (July 2008): 545–74.

10. Some economists agree. Wendy Liebmann, a retail and marketing consultant, is quoted as saying: "Some of the same major retailers that rushed to create one-stop shopping environments are now realizing that there is growing opportunity for the small stores." Quoted in Stephanie Anderson Forest, "Look Who's Thinking Small: Mega-retailers Are Finding Main Street May Be Paved with Gold," http.businessweek.com/1999/99_20/b3629080.htm. In an attempt to address this need, big box retailer Walmart has opened a chain of small neighborhood markets. Sarah Coffey, "'Mini' Wal-Mart, Coming to a City Near You," http.walletpop.com/blog/2010/04/28/mini-wal-mart-coming-to-a-city-near-you.

11. See Kenneth E. Stone, "Competing with Discount Mass Merchandisers" (paper, Iowa State University, 1995), www.econ.iastate.edu/faculty/stone/1995_IA_WM_Study.pdf; "Retail Expert Sees a Shift Back to Main Street," *New Urban News* (December 1999), www.gibbsplanning.com/nun.html; Steven Lagerfeld, "What Main Street Can Learn from the Mall," *Atlantic Monthly*, October 13, 2002; and Anne Field, "Small Shops See Smallness as Their Big Selling Point," *New York Times*, December 15, 2007, B1.

12. Palm Beach, Florida, requires proposed uses to submit evidence that not less than 50 percent of the customers will be local residents (Zoning Ordinance, Section 134-1107); and Peoria, Illinois, permits retail and office uses that serve residents in the adjacent residential area (Peoria Code, Section 3.17). Washington, D.C., limits eating and drinking establishments to no more than 25 percent of the linear street frontage (Municipal Regulations, Title 11, Rule 1302.5). San Francisco permits commercial uses less than 2,000 square feet and will not approve uses greater than 4,000 square feet (Zoning Ordinance, Section 722.21). Santa Monica, California, permits commercial uses that do not exceed 3,000 square feet (Municipal Code 9.04.14.080). Palm Beach, Florida, permits commercial uses less than 2,000 square feet (Zoning Ordinance, Section 134-1107). It is reevaluating the 2,000 square feet requirement because small stores are losing out to bigger stores in the nearby county. Paul Castro, private discussion with author, August 6, 2010. Palm Beach, Florida, excludes "formula restaurants"—that is, it excludes a restaurant if it is "one of a

group of three or more restaurants in the nation, and with similar name, standardized menus, exterior design, and uniforms" (Section 134-1107). The City of Calistoga, California, also prohibits formula restaurants (Calistoga Municipal Code, Titles 17.04.61 and 17.22.040D). Excluding chains can be contentious. Landlords find chains to be reliable, long-term tenants. Those who object to chains tend to be affluent shoppers; low-income shoppers tend to favor the lower prices offered by the chains and welcome them, especially if products are of a higher quality than the ones to which shoppers are accustomed. See Michael J. Berne, "Balancing Chains and Independents" (paper presented at the National Main Street Conference, Baltimore, May 2005); and Stacy Mitchell, *The Hometown Advantage: How to Defend Your Main Street Against Chain Stores . . . And Why It Matters* (Minneapolis: Institute for Local Self Reliance, 2000).

13. The material in this section is based on Sidney Brower, "The Feasibility of Mixed-income Communities" (study presented at IAPS-CSBE Network and the IAPS Housing Network international symposium, Istanbul, Turkey, 2009). It draws on three reports produced by students in the Urban Studies and Planning Program at the University of Maryland: "Building Community: Jonestown, Albemarle Square, and the Legacy of Flag House Courts" (2007); "Heritage Crossing at 5: Successes and Challenges in a HOPE VI Development" (2008); and "Broadway Overlook" (2009).

   Emily Talen suggests that social diversity in a neighborhood can be achieved by increasing suburban densities, and by varying lot sizes and building types. She does not claim that diversity results in a cohesive community. Emily Talen, *Design for Diversity* (Oxford: Elsevier, 2008).

14. William J. Wilson, *The Truly Disadvantaged: The Inner City, the Underclass, and Public Policy* (Chicago: University of Chicago Press, 1987).

15. Mark L. Joseph, "Is Mixed-income Development an Antidote to Urban Poverty?" *Housing Policy Debate* 17, no. 2 (2006): 209–34.

16. New Urbanism is an urban design movement that emerged in the United States in the early 1980s and promotes walkable neighborhoods. Its organizing body is the Congress for the New Urbanism, founded in 1993. Congress for the New Urbanism, Charter of the New Urbanism, principle 4, under "The Neighborhood, the

District, and the Corridor" (1996), available online at www.cnu .org/charter.

17. U.S. Department of Housing and Urban Development, "HOPE VI: Community Building Makes a Difference" (2000), www .huduser.org/portal/publications/pubasst/hope.html.

18. One development has 336 units, of which 54 percent are rental; another has 260 units, with 29 percent rental; and the third has 132 units, with 66 percent rental.

19. Gans, "Balanced Community"; Rapoport, "Neighborhood Heterogeneity or Homogeneity."

20. For example, Gans, *Levittowners.*

21. The Baltimore case studies are not necessarily typical of mixed income developments in other cities; however, it is precisely because they lack the conditions that generate community that they draw attention to what these conditions are.

22. A delegation of residents visits each newcomer with a package of information about the community—such as local practices and expectations, how to get services, and how to join the community association—and frequently a gift of flowers, a cake, or cookies.

23. This discussion draws on the reports of four studies of Patterson Park: Planning Studio, "Patterson Park: Putting the Pieces Together" (Urban Studies and Planning Program, University of Maryland, 1994); Baltimore City Department of Recreation and Parks, and Urban Studies and Planning Program, "Patterson Park—How People Use It and Feel About It: Overview and Summary of the 1995 Survey" (Urban Studies and Planning Program, University of Maryland, 1996); Sidney Brower and Erica Todd, "Community Participation in the Plan for Patterson Park: An Assessment" (Urban Studies and Planning Program, University of Maryland, 1998); and Sidney Brower and Nkechi Hislop, "User Survey of Patterson Park 2008" (Urban Studies and Planning Program, University of Maryland, 2008).

24. Planning Studio, "Patterson Park."

25. The work was assisted by an Urban Service grant from the U.S. Department of Education to the Urban Studies and Planning Program, University of Maryland.

26. Rhodeside & Harwell, Master Plan for Patterson Park, Maryland, Baltimore Department of Recreation and Parks (August 1998).

27. Ford, in *The Trouble with City Planning* (New Haven, Conn: Yale University Press, 2010), argues that effective resident participation

results in a plan that people can understand and that addresses what they consider to be important issues.

28. Brower and Hislop, "User Survey."

29. Ibid., 36, 20.

30. Emily Talen, "New Urbanism, Social Equity, and the Challenge of Post-Katrina Rebuilding in Mississippi," *Journal of Planning Education and Research* 27 (2008): 277–93.

INDEX